Archaeology

Teacher Edition

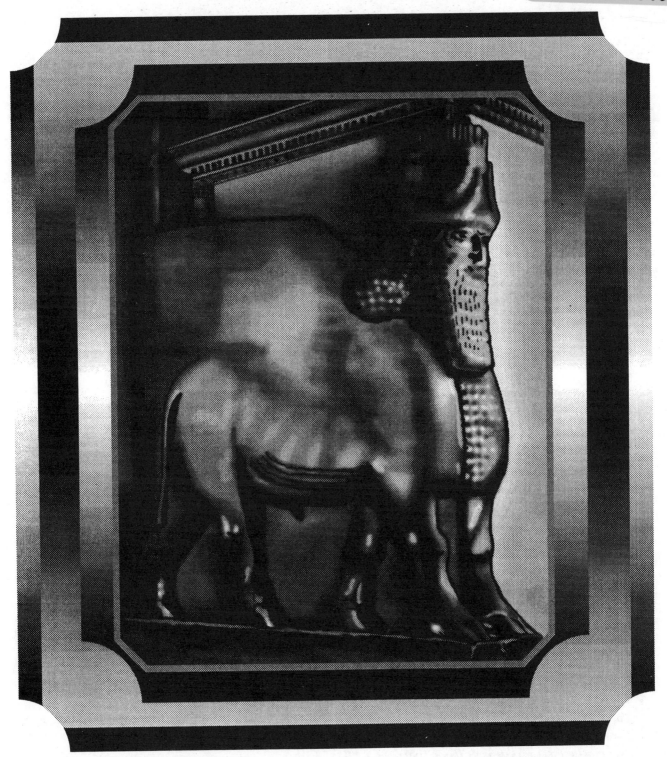

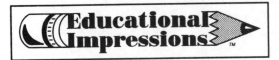

Written by Rebecca Stark
Illustrated by Karen Birchak
and Nelsy Fontalvo

Explanation of Cover Design

In 1845 Sir Austen Layard began excavation at Numrud. He discovered the remains of palaces from the ninth and seventh centuries BC. Perhaps the most valuable find was this huge statue of a winged bull.

ISBN 1-56644-091-2

© 2001 Educational Impressions, Inc.

Printed in the U.S.A.

EDUCATIONAL IMPRESSIONS, INC.
Hawthorne, New Jersey 07507

Table of Contents

To the Teacher

The ancient world has a great deal to teach us. Its achievements in literature, art, philosophy and religion were remarkable. The objective of this book is to introduce students to the various civilizations and to acquaint them with these fantastic achievements. It is also intended that students gain an appreciation for and an understanding of these and other cultures which are different from their own and that they come to understand the need to respect these differences. It is hoped that students will recognize the fact that in spite of vast differences among cultures that all peoples have certain needs that remain the same.

The self-directed activities emphasize higher-level thinking skills and the activities have been keyed to Bloom's taxonomy for your convenience. Although not so marked, other higher-level skills, such as fluency, originality, and risk-taking are also encouraged.

I hope you and your students enjoy your trip back in time to these ancient worlds!

Bloom's Taxonomy

KNOWLEDGE (K): The recall of specifics and universals; bringing to mind the appropriate material.

COMPREHENSION (C): Understanding what is being communicated and making use of what is being communicated without necessarily relating it to other material or seeing its fullest implications.

APPLICATION (AP): The use of abstractions in particular and concrete situations. The abstractions may be in the form of general or technical ideas, rules, or methods which must be remembered and applied.

ANALYSIS (AN): Breaking down a communication into its constituent elements or parts so that the relative hierarchy of ideas expressed are made explicit.

SYNTHESIS (S): Putting together elements and parts to form a whole; arranging and combining the elements in a pattern or structure not clearly there before.

EVALUATION (E): Making judgments about the extent to which material and methods satisfy criteria, either given to the student or determined by the student.

Benjamin Bloom. *Taxonomy of Educational Objectives. Handbook 1: Cognitive Domain.* New York: David Mc Kay, 1956.

What Is Archaeology?

Archaeology is the systematic retrieval and study of the material remains of past human life and culture. The word itself comes from two Greek words: *arkhaios,* meaning "old," and *logos,* meaning "theory" or "science." The remains that archaeologists study include a wide variety of things, from the simplest tools to the most beautiful palaces and cathedrals. In fact, they include everything made by human beings. These objects produced or shaped by human workmanship are called **artifacts.** Archaeologists are descriptive workers. It is their job to describe, classify and analyze the artifacts they find.

Throughout the years diligent archaeologists have collected and studied millions of artifacts from virtually every part of the world. It is to these men and women that we owe much of our knowledge about the lifestyles of the people who made those artifacts. We especially must thank them for our knowledge of prehistoric times, for without their findings, we would know little of those cultures.

What Is Culture?

The knowledge, beliefs, art and institutions along with any other products of human workmanship and thought are commonly known as a society's culture. People in different societies have different ways of doing things and different ways of interpreting the world around them. We say, therefore, that they have different cultures. These cultures are named either from a characteristic feature or from the place where they existed.

At one time archaeologists thought that inventions were made in one place and then brought from place to place through trade or other contacts with new places. This is known as **diffusion.** While some diffusion undoubtedly took place, it was probably the exception rather than the rule. Most likely, the same inventions were made over and over again in different parts of the world as a result of similar problems and situations.

Where to Dig

The artifacts archaeologists search for are often buried and must be dug up, or excavated. That's why an archaeological expedition is often called a **dig**.

1. Ruins that can be seen were the first sites to be explored. Name at least three examples in which at least part of an artifact (for example, a monument) could be seen without digging. (K, C)

_____

_____

_____

_____

Archaeologists look for mounds that look different from natural hills. In the Near East many of these mounds, called **tells,** can be found. As houses collapsed (or towns destroyed), they were leveled off. New houses (or towns) were later built on top of the debris or on the layer of soil that had formed.

2. Draw a diagram of a tell. (K, C, AP)

3. In many cases, when a town was destroyed by a disaster, years later people again settled at the same site. Explain. (C, AN)

_____

_____

_____

_____

Modern Aids

The use of aerial photography in archaeological explorations began during World War I and increased greatly after World War II.

4. Evaluate the importance of aerial photography in archaeology. (K, C, AN, E)

_____

_____

_____

_____

5. Sometimes an aerial view shows that in certain areas of a field the crops are growing more or less luxuriantly than in others. What might each of these conditions mean? Draw a diagram to illustrate your explanation. (K, C, AP, AN)

_____

_____

_____

_____

6. Research one of the following and explain how it helps archaeologists decide upon a site: proton magnetometer, resistivity surveying, closed circuit TV or another modern invention. (K, C, AN)

_____

_____

_____

_____

_____

_____

Stratigraphy:
Digging out a Site Layer by Layer

Stratigraphy is the method of digging out a site layer by layer. Each layer, or *stratum*, is a settlement within a certain culture and represents a different way of life.

Steps:

1. Make a trial trench by slicing down through the mounds as if it were a cake.

2. Search for the following clues as to the site's history: differences in color; differences in building materials; traces of flood, fire or other disasters; and holes made by posts which have since rotted away.

3. If the site seems to have possibilities, begin excavation.

4. Record in detail what you find, stratum by stratum.

5. Be sure to read the layers in their correct order. If the levels have not been disturbed, the top layer will be your most recent and the bottom stratum will be the oldest.

1. What might cause a mix-up in your layers? (C, AN, E)

_____

_____

This is the artist's conception of stratigraphy. Fill in artifacts that might be found in the stratum from the twentieth and twenty-first centuries.

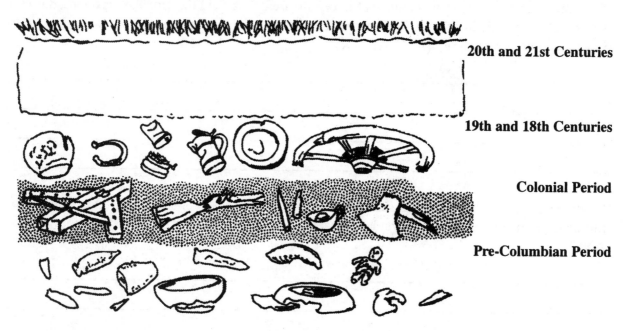

20th and 21st Centuries

19th and 18th Centuries

Colonial Period

Pre-Columbian Period

2. What kinds of artifacts do you think will survive for future archaeologists? Explain. (C, AP, AN)

_____

_____

Excavation

Many digs are carried out by the grid method of excavation. The mound is pegged with string into numbered squares. Each square corresponds to a square on a map of the site. The workers then dig a shallow pit in each square, leaving a raised area to outline each square. A pattern of horizontal and vertical lines which form uniform squares is called a **grid.** Each find must be identified with its level and square.

The three-dimensional system of recording was developed by General Pitt-Rivers in the 1880s. He set a new standard of keeping carefully detailed notes and records while excavating prehistoric and Roman settlements in England. Although today all archaeologists keep meticulous records, such efficiency was rare in his time.

1. Make a grid representing your bedroom. Include a record of all the items in the room. (AP)

2. List at least three synonyms for *meticulous*. What adjectives might be used to describe the grid method of excavation. (K, C)

_____

_____

Tools

Here are some tools used by the archaeologist at a dig.

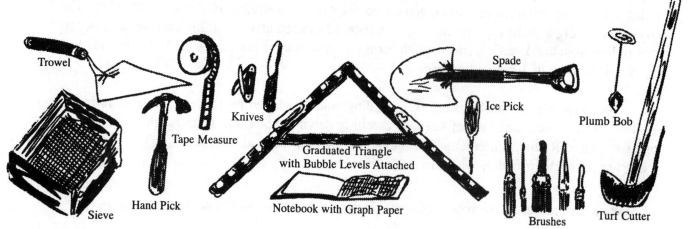

1. When an archaeologist (or a helper) finds an artifact, he or she changes to a finer tool, such as a knife or an ice pick. Why? (C)

_____

_____

2. Nothing is thrown away until the archaeologist has carefully checked it. All the soil is sifted through a wire-meshed sieve. For what purpose? (C)

_____

_____

_____

3. Suppose you were an amateur archaeologist along on a dig. You found what appears to be an entire vase. What would you do and why? (AN, E)

_____

_____

_____

4. When an artifact is found, it is measured or photographed *in situ,* exactly where and how it was found. Why is it important to photograph and record things *in situ?* (C, AN)

_____

_____

_____

Potsherds

Potsherds are bits of shattered pottery.

1. Analyze the following statement: Because pottery was of so little value to the ancients, it is of great value to the archaeologists. (AN, E)

_____

_____

_____

2. How can we learn about the lifestyles and beliefs of ancient people from their pottery? Cite an example. (C, AN)

_____

_____

_____

If pottery is found in more than one layer of a site, a pottery sequence can be set up. The sequence can then be used to compare the ages of the settlements in that area.

Sometimes a problem arises. Suppose an archaeologist encounters the following situation:

    1. There are two sets of ruins.

    2. In each town the people had dug pits into which they threw their rubbish.

Second Level ————————————

First Level ————————————

3. Unless the archaeologist notices the slight differences in the soil, what mistake might he or she make? (C, AN)

_____

_____

_____

The Ages of Human Existence

The Ages of Human Existence are based upon the tools that were made during each age.

Prehistoric Humans

From the time humans first appeared on Earth they made things. At first they probably used soft materials, such as wood or bone, that bend easily. Then they learned to fashion tools from flint (a fine-grained quartz) by chipping off the edges. As time went on they learned to use other materials. Much of what archaeologists learned about prehistoric humans came from the stone artifacts they found; therefore, prehistoric times were called the Stone Age. Scholars later divided the Stone Age into two distinct periods: the Paleolithic, or Old Stone, Age and the Neolithic, or New Stone, Age.

Some of the most fantastic discoveries of the Stone Age have been made by L. S. B. Leakey, an English anthropologist. Among his finds were the stone tools and skeletal remains of early human beings which date back two million years. They were found in Tanzania.

The Paleolithic (Old Stone) Age: During this age people were merely food finders. They had crude stone tools with which to protect themselves.

The Neolithic (Old Stone) Age: During this age people began to produce food. They discovered farming and learned to tame animals. Polished stone tools were made during this period.

Civilization

Civilization was born in the Near East about 5,000 years ago with the rise of Sumer in the valley of the Tigris and Euphrates rivers. (It came to Egypt slightly later.) In most places civilization was accompanied by two inventions: **writing** and **metallurgy** (the process of removing metal from ore). Metallurgy, of course, led to the making of metal **tools.**

The ages of human existence continue to be classified according to the tools that were made. At first tools were made out of copper, but pure copper is too soft to be effective. Eventually, people learned to harden it with alloys.

The Bronze Age: The true formula for bronze, 90% copper and 10% tin, was first discovered late in the third millennium BC. (A millennium is a span of 1,000 years.)

The Iron Age: Archaeologists generally date the beginning of the Iron Age at about 1200 BC. The art of smelting iron seems to have been discovered in the Taurus Mountains of Asia Minor, where ore was plentiful.

1. What is the name sometimes given to the age in which we live? (K)

_____

2. Archaeologists use these ages to classify settlements. Explain why it is not possible to use these ages as a guide to exact dates. (C)

_____

_____

_____

_____

_____

Chronology

There are two kinds of chronology: absolute and relative. It is called **absolute chronology** when the dating can be verified—for example, according to written records. It is called **relative chronology** when the dating cannot be substantiated by written records or other certain methods. Instead, it must be compared to other things found nearby.

It is important for an archaeologist to note the objects with which an artifact is found as well as its exact location. What is found with it is often a clue to its age.

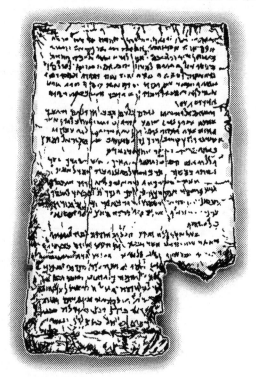

Match the Experts

1. Match the finds on the left with the expert on the right who might help an archaeologist date a find. (C, AN)

____ Paintings of animals
on a cave wall

1. Chemist

____ Pottery in which pollen was used
to temper the clay

2. Linguist

____ A piece of vase, ground into powder,
to be tested for the glow it gives off

3. Paleontologist

____ A tablet with ancient writings
on it

4. Geologist

____ Human remains left by retreating
glacier of last Ice Age

5. Botanist

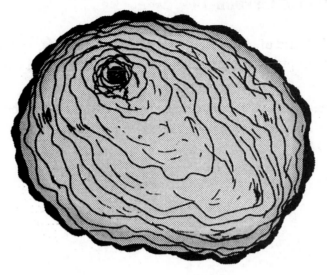

Dendrochronology

In the American Southwest the difference between the wet and dry seasons causes a pattern in the annual growth rings of trees. The counting of the growth rings of trees to date past events is called **dendrochronology.**

The Varve System

In Scandinavia dating is sometimes based on the number of **varves,** or annual layers of sediment, in glacial lakes.

2. What are the disadvantages of dating methods such as dendrochronology and the varve system? (C, AN)

_____

_____

_____

Carbon-14 Dating

All living organisms contain a small amount of a radioactive element known as carbon-14. (Radioactive means that it has the power to give off the type of energy called radiation.) While the organism is alive, it absorbs new carbon-14 at the same rate that it loses the carbon-14 it already had absorbed. (It turns into ordinary carbon.)

The reason carbon-14 is useful in dating is that once an organism has died, it no longer absorbs new carbon-14; moreover, it continues to lose the carbon-14 it had already absorbed. The rate at which it loses the carbon-14 is known; therefore, by measuring the amount of carbon-14, scientists can determine the appropriate age of the object made with that material.

Rate of Disintegration of Carbon-14

Carbon-14 has a half-life of about 5,700 years. In other words, 5,700 years after its death, half of the carbon-14 atoms present in the animal or vegetable material will have disintegrated.

3. Which of the following artifacts could be dated by the carbon-14 method? (C)

____ papyrus scrolls

____ a bone knife

____ a metal knife

____ a wooden statue

____ the Sphinx

____ a wooden beam

____ the Aztec Stone Calendar

____ linen cloth used to wrap the Dead Sea Scrolls

4. Assume that the following diagram represents the amount of radiation from a wooden beam that was just cut from a live tree.

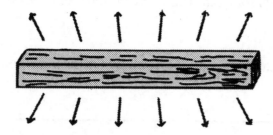

Approximately how old is this beam cut from a similar kind of tree? (C)

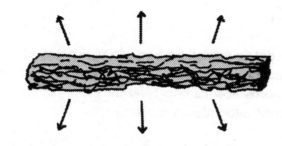

The beam is about _____ years old.

Ancient Egypt

The Pyramids

In Egypt are massive monuments called **pyramids.** They have a rectangular base and four triangular sides, meeting in a single point at the top. Over eighty of these structures have been found along the Nile River, all on the western bank, where the sun sets.

Why were they built? Well, to understand why they were built, you first have to understand the Egyptians' belief in an afterlife. To the ancient Egyptians, life after death was more important than their present lives. It was, therefore, very important that when a person died, especially a person as important as a pharaoh, the body be preserved and protected.

To preserve the bodies, a system of embalming and drying, called **mummification,** was practiced. The heart was left in the body, but the other organs were placed in objects called **canopic jars.** The body was washed with wine and spices and covered with salts. It was left for up to seventy days to dry. Then it was placed in a royal coffin and laid to rest in a tomb.

In the case of the pharaohs, however, ordinary tombs were not enough. The pharaohs were the first real kings in the world. Before them, men had ruled over a certain town or a certain tribe. The pharaohs were the first to rule over an entire country. Because they were so powerful, they were able to demand the construction of the magnificent tombs we call the pyramids. All the things the pharaoh would need in his afterlife were placed in the pyramid with him: clothing, furniture, model boats, models of servants—anything at all that he might need. The halls were decorated with scenes which depicted the pharaoh's life.

The largest of all the pyramids was the great pyramid of Khufu (called Cheops by the Greeks), which was built at Gizeh. Called one of the Seven Wonders of the World by the ancient Greeks, it was an amazing architectural feat. About 2,300,000 blocks of stone, each averaging about two and one-half tons, were used. As there were no quarries nearby, the blocks had to be quarried in an area about 500 miles away and floated down the Nile River. According to the Greek historian Herodotus, it took approximately 100,000 men about twenty years to build it. Unfortunately, robbers destroyed the tomb and stole all they could. They even destroyed the mummy to be sure that the pharaoh's Ka, or spirit, couldn't take revenge. Later kings decided instead to bury their tombs in the area that is now known as the Valley of the Kings.

Egyptology, the study of the culture and artifacts of ancient Egypt, actually began with Napoleon's invasion of Egypt in 1798. Early excavations, however, were more of a search for treasures than true archaeology. In fact, the demand for Egyptian antiquities—objects from ancient times—led to a great deal of tomb robbing.

The founding of the Antiquities Service of Egypt in 1858 by the French scholar Auguste Mariette put an end to most of the pillaging. Although this marked the beginning of controlled research, it was the British archaeologist Sir Flinders Petrie, who began his work in Egypt in 1880, who truly developed a systematic method of excavation.

1. Draw a map of Egypt and indicate the location of the Great Pyramid of Khufu. (K, C, AP)

2. Make a flipbook of the Seven Wonders of the Ancient World. (K, C, AP)

3. In spite of the immense strength and permanence of the pyramids, they did not serve their purpose. Explain. (C, AN)

_____

_____

_____

_____

_____

4. Use the religious beliefs of the ancient Egyptians to explain why so many artifacts have been found in Egypt. (C, AP)

_____

_____

_____

_____

_____

5. In most places an archaeologist must base his or her study upon scraps of stone, bone, pottery and metal. Things made of wood, leather, hair, linen and other materials that were once alive turn to dust within a few centuries. Analyze the conditions in Egypt that make it an exception. (AN)

_____

_____

_____

_____

6. Paint a mural in the Egyptian style with scenes that depict the daily life of the President of the United States or of another important official. (C, AP, AN)

7. When Flinders Petrie was still a young boy of about eight, he made the following statement regarding the proper method of excavation: "The earth ought to be pared away inch by inch to see all that is in it and how it lies." Research the early methods of excavation being practiced at the time Petrie made this statement (early 1860s) and evaluate the statement in terms of what you learn. (C, AP, AN, E)

_____

_____

_____

8. Near the pyramids is a monument called the Sphinx. Out of clay, make a model of the Sphinx. (K, AP, S)

The Rosetta Stone

In 1779 one of Napoleon's officers discovered a large, irregularly-shaped, black basalt tablet near the town of Rosetta, about thirty miles from Alexandria. On the tablet was an inscription in three alphabets: **Greek, Egyptian hieroglyphic** and **demotic,** a cursive form of hieroglyphics. The inscription was a decree passed by Egyptian priests at Memphis in 196 BC, during the reign of Ptolemy V. The Ptolemies, Macedonian Greeks, ruled in Egypt after Alexander the Great overthrew the Persians and added Egypt to his empire. This **Rosetta Stone,** as it came to be known, led to the eventual decipherment of hieroglyphics.

The Greek, of course, could be read by the scholars. The problem was in figuring out the meaning of the hieroglyphics. Most of those who had previously tried to decipher the symbols thought that they were merely pictures of the words for which they stood. One by one, they gave up their work in frustration.

Much of the credit for the solving of the puzzle must go to an Englishman, Thomas Young. Young realized that the hieroglyphics had advanced from the stage of picture writing; he believed that the symbols represented sounds. Young also figured out that the Egyptians wrote royal names within ovals, called **cartouches.** He assumed that the names Ptolemy and Cleopatra, found in the Greek inscriptions, would also be found in the cartouches in the hieroglyphic section. He guessed that these names would be written in symbols that had the same phonetic values as the Greek. Young never completely deciphered the hieroglyphics, but he did figure out a few of the symbols by working with the two names, Ptolemy and Cleopatra. Also, he determined the way in which the symbols were to be read.

Although Young did not complete the task, a brilliant young French scholar, Jean-François Champollion, started out where Young had left off. Champollion was able to work out the alphabetic sounds for the hieroglyphic symbols in the names. He continued to work on the project of deciphering the hieroglyphics for many years. In 1822 he compiled an entire list of hieroglyphics and their Greek equivalents. He was the first to realize that some of the signs were alphabetic, some were syllabic and others were determinative, meaning that they stood for an idea or an object.

It is to Thomas Young and Jean-François Champollion that the world owes much of its knowledge about ancient Egypt, for it was the diligent work of these two men that led to the translation of all other hieroglyphic texts.

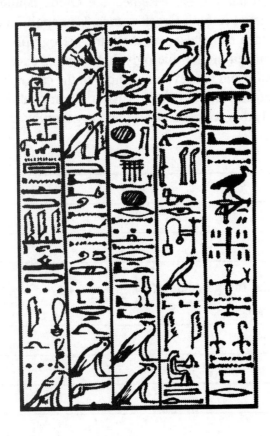

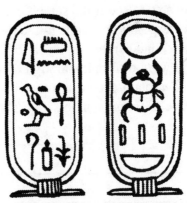

These cartouches show the names of Tutankhamen before and after his coronation: Nebkheprure and Tutankhamen.

1. Show how Champollion used the cartouches of Ptolemy and Cleopatra. Use the similar sounds in each to figure out which hieroglyphic sounds stood for sounds similar to the Greek counterparts. (C, AP)

The first cartouche belongs to Ptolemy and the second to Cleopatra:

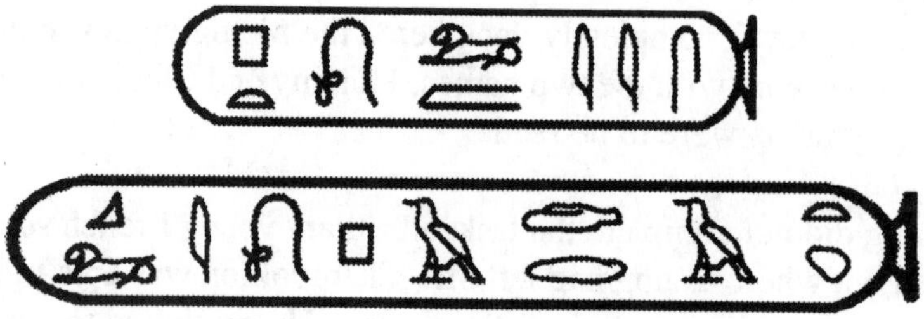

Note: Young had already figured out that two small signs, , were used to indicate that the name was feminine.

2. Where a sound appeared in one name only, Champollion assigned the Greek sound and assumed it was correct. For the sounds that appeared in both Greek names, Champollion compared the sets to see if the same Greek sound in each name also had the same hieroglyph. Each of the corresponding sounds in the two names matched in their hieroglyphic symbols except one set. The second symbol in the cartouche for Ptolemy and the seventh symbol in the cartouche for Cleopatra were different although they had the same sound in Greek. Champollion made a suggestion to explain this occurrence and turned out to be correct. Can you suggest why the two might have different symbols? (C, AN)

3. Give an example in our alphabet where a similar thing occurs. (K)

4. In addition to studying the Rosetta Stone, Young and Champollion studied other artifacts. One artifact that was very helpful was an obelisk found at Philae, Egypt. Draw a picture of an obelisk. (C, AP)

5. Why was the inscription on the Rosetta Stone written in both Greek and Egyptian? (C)

_____

_____

_____

_____

6. Most early records of the ancient Egyptians were inscribed in stone or clay. Then they invented papyrus, a paperlike material made from river reeds. Research the steps that must be taken in making papyrus. Make a chart. (C, AP)

7. Analyze the importance of the fact that the Rosetta Stone included an inscription in Greek. (AN, E)

_____

_____

_____

_____

8. Invent a new language with an original alphabet. Write a message in English and in your new language. Be sure to include some names that are transliterated into the new language according to English phonetic values. Then write another message in your new language. Have a classmate try to decipher the second message. (S)

9. Evaluate the impact of the Rosetta Stone upon our knowledge of ancient Egyptian civilization. (E)

_____

_____

_____

_____

The Tomb of King Tutankhamen

One of the most remarkable discoveries—if not *the* most remarkable—was the finding of King Tutankhamen's tomb by British archaeologist Howard Carter.

In the early 1900s a wealthy Englishman, Lord Carnarvon, became interested in archaeology. In 1906 he was granted a permit to excavate in Egypt, provided an expert supervised the work; the expert he chose was Howard Carter. In 1907 a partnership began that would one day make worldwide headlines!

Although most archaeologists believed there was no longer anything to be found in the Valley of the Kings, Carter did not. His persistence and excellent judgment of the little evidence he found kept him going. He was sure "there were tombs concealed by the dumps left by previous excavators, which had never been properly examined."

In 1917 Carter began his work in the Valley. He made a map of the Valley and divided it into sections. As the search of each section was completed, he marked the area on the map. This ensured that no piece of the Valley would be left unexamined.

Years passed, but he did not give up. He was certain that the tomb of one king, at least, was still to be found. He based this belief on the fact that in 1907 an excavator had found several clay jars with seal impressions including the name of Tutankhamen. They appeared to have been used during the funeral ceremonies of Tutankhamen, the "boy king" who ruled more than 3,000 years ago.

Lord Carnarvon

In the summer of 1922 Lord Carnarvon told Carter that he could no longer subsidize the undertaking. Carter showed him the map and explained that he had examined the entire Valley except for one small area. He begged for one more season to complete his work. Lord Carnarvon agreed.

On November 4, 1922, Howard Carter arrived at the site and found his workers silently awaiting him. They had found a step cut into the rock. By the next day, enough debris had been cleared away to be sure it was a tomb. But was it a finished tomb? Was it a royal tomb? Even if it was a royal tomb, was anything of value left in it? After all, every royal tomb found so far by archaeologists had been looted of all its valuables!

On November 6 Howard Carter found at the bottom of sixteen steps a sealed doorway with the name Tutankhamen. Using a remarkable amount of self-control, he refilled the stairway, posted a guard and sent the following telegram to his patron, Lord Carnarvon: "AT LAST YOU HAVE MADE A WONDERFUL DISCOVERY IN THE VALLEY. A MAGNIFICENT TOMB WITH SEALS INTACT. RE-COVERED SAME FOR YOUR ARRIVAL. CONGRATULATIONS CARTER."

When Lord Carnarvon and his daughter arrived at the site on November 23, work once again began. Soon it became clear that the seals at the bottom of the tomb had at one time been broken and that someone had entered the tomb after the burial; however, Carter was encouraged by the fact that whoever entered the tomb also bothered to re-seal the tomb upon leaving. Only time would tell.

On November 28 they found a second sealed doorway. On the seals were impressions of the name Tutankhamen. Carter made a tiny hole in the upper left-hand corner and inserted a candle. After a few moments Lord Carnarvon anxiously asked, "Can you see anything?" and Carter nervously replied, "Yes, wonderful things."

It took ten seasons to finish the work there, but Howard Carter's great manual skill, tremendous patience and outstanding draftsmanship paid off. At last his task was complete. All had been cleared and the treasures preserved and removed to the National Museum in Cairo for the world to gaze upon in amazement.

1. List the kinds of details that Carter had to include on each index card he prepared for the artifacts he found. (K, C)

1. _____   4. _____

2. _____   5. _____

3. _____   6. _____

2. What clue inspired Carter to search for Tutankhamen's tomb? (C)

_____

_____

_____

3. Make a poster advertising an upcoming exhibit of the treasures of Tutankhamen to entice people to visit in spite of the long waiting lines. (AP, E)

4. Carter took months to photograph, label, mend, pack and ship the contents of the first room. On one side of the room stood two statues facing each other with a sealed doorway between them. He knew that there must be other rooms beyond that doorway and that in one of those rooms most likely would be King Tutankhamen himself! Yet he waited to complete the first room before breaking down the doorway. What does this tell use about the character of Howard Carter? (AN)

_____

_____

_____

_____

5. Lord Carnarvon and Howard Carter disagreed over what should be done with the artifacts they found. Carter thought all should be given to the Cairo Museum. Carnarvon wanted to retain some of the less important ones for the expedition. Choose a point of view and prepare a speech for a debate taking that point of view. Then prepare a speech taking the opposite point of view. (AN, S, E)

6. Pretend that you are Howard Carter. Write an entry in your diary after you send Lord Carnarvon the telegram. (AN, E)

Dear Diary,

_____

_____

_____

_____

_____

_____

_____

_____

_____

_____

_____

_____

_____

_____

_____

7. List three synonyms for *perseverance*. Tell why perseverance is an important trait for an archaeologist. (K, C, AN)

_____

_____

_____

_____

Future Artifacts

Archaeologists often look in burial grounds for artifacts, for many ancient peoples believed in an afterlife in which their future would be much more like their present. For example, an earthly warrior would become a spirit warrior.

1. Suppose you believed in an afterlife. Draw a picture that shows the objects you would want to have buried with you so that you could carry on as in your present life. (K, C, AP)

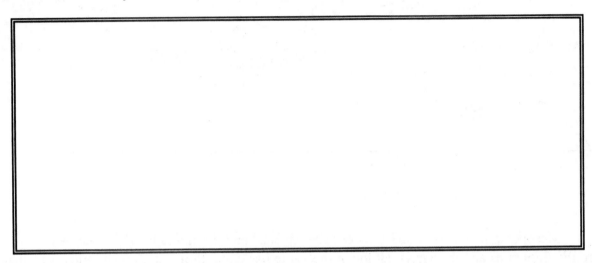

2. What objects might the following people want to have buried with them? (C, K, AP)

A lawyer? _____

A doctor? _____

An author? _____

3. Suppose the custom of burying objects with the dead were still followed. Choose one of the above professions or another of your choice and draw a picture of the artifacts that might be found in his or her tomb 1,000 years from now. (C, AP, AN)

Mesopotamia

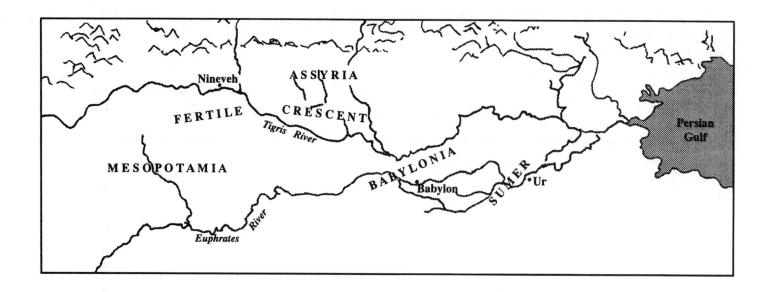

Mesopotamia means "Land Between the Rivers," and the rivers to which the name refers are the Euphrates and the Tigris, although the name has come to mean a much larger area than just that. Mesopotamia had many languages, many cultures, and no permanent capital city. It gave rise to a number of civilizations, among them being the civilization of Sumer, believed to be the oldest civilization in the world. The Sumerians developed an urban society in southern Mesopotamia in the beginning of the third millennium BC. It was followed in the latter part of the millennium by the Akkadian Empire and the Ur III Empire. They were succeeded by the Old Babylonian Empire (2017–1794 BC), the Assyrian Empire (1100–612 BC) and the Neo-Babylonian Empire (sixth century BC), which spread Mesopotamian influence throughout the Near East.

1. What is the present name for most of the area once called Mesopotamia? (K) _____

Clay

In no other civilization in the world has clay played such an important role as in Mesopotamia. As there was no easily accessible source of stone, the architecture was almost exclusively mud-brick. Clay was used for statues and other forms of artwork as well as for such common objects as jars and other pottery. Clay was also used as seals for the jars, on which impressions could be made to show ownership. But most importantly, clay became the vehicle for impressing signs with established meanings. In other words, the use of clay led to the invention of writing. This writing was an important part of all aspects of life in Mesopotamia; it was especially important to the development of literature. For although the literature is still being studied and translated, scholars have deciphered enough to know that the literature of Mesopotamia was one of its greatest cultural achievements.

Cuneiform Writing

The oldest written material yet discovered is from the Sumerian city of Uruk (Ereck). It dates from before 3000 BC. We call Mesopotamian writing **"cuneiform,"** which means "wedge-shaped." The wedge-shaped characters were inscribed on tablets of soft clay.

Just as the Rosetta Stone was the key to Egyptian hieroglyphics, the Behistun Rock, a monument to King Darius of Persia, was the key to cuneiform writing. The Rock of Behistun also had a triple inscription: Old Persian, Elamite and Babylonian. It was Sir Henry Rawlinson whose success in deciphering the Old Persian portion (1937) provided the key to the deciphering of Mesopotamian cuneiform script by himself and other scholars by 1857.

2. As a young man, British army officer Henry Rawlinson risked his life to study the inscription of the Behistun Rock. Research his method and draw a sketch to show how he accomplished his task. (C, AP)

3. Explain why the tell, or mound of occupational debris, is the characteristic ruin form of Mesopotamia. (C, AN)

_____

_____

_____

_____

Paul-Émile Botta

In 1842 French consul Paul-Émile Botta was sent to Mosul and assigned to explore the vanishing cities of Assyria. At that time all that was known of them was from conflicting accounts of ancient writers and from biblical references. He began to excavate at Kuyunjik but abandoned it for what seemed to be better prospects at Khorsabad. It was at Khorsabad in 1843 that Botta made his fantastic discovery of the palace of the Assyrian King Sargon II. Sargon II reigned from 722 BC to 705 BC and was the father of Sennacherib. As Paul Botta himself explained, he was the first person of his time to gaze upon the remains of a civilization that had been hinted at in the Old Testament.

4. Among the ruins uncovered by Paul Botta were the remains of a ziggurat. A **ziggurat** is a staged tower in which each story is smaller than the one below. Its name comes from the Assyrian word meaning "height." Make a model ziggurat. (C, AP)

Sir Austen Layard

The excavations in Mesopotamia by Sir Austen Henry Layard taught us much about Assyrian and Babylonian culture. As a young boy, Layard became interested in the area because of the stories he had read in *Arabian Nights*. In 1839, at twenty-two years of age, Layard left his position as apprentice in a London law office and set out on his journey on horseback to Mesopotamia. In 1843 Layard was employed by the ambassador at Istanbul for unofficial diplomatic missions. His work took him to Mosul, Iraq. While there, he became increasingly interested in finding the great biblical cities. In 1845 he began excavation of Numrud, which Layard mistook for Ninevah. What he discovered were the remains of palaces from the ninth and seventh centuries BC. Included among his finds were many sculptures and other valuable pieces of artwork. Perhaps the single most valuable object was a huge winged bull. In the following few years Layard excavated several sites. In 1849 he began to dig at Kuyunjik, the mound opposite Mosul on the eastern bank of the Tigris. Paul-Émile Botta had done some work there but had abandoned the site. It was at Kuyunjik that Layard found Ninevah and uncovered the palace of Sennacherib. Although many important artifacts were found there, the most important were undoubtedly the large number of cuneiform tablets from the state archives. It was from these tablets that we learned much of what we know about Assyrian and Babylonian culture.

5. How do you think Layard's Arabian workers felt when they first uncovered the statue of the winged bull and saw its head rising from the earth? (AN)

_____

_____

_____

_____

Ur

One of the most impressive discoveries in Mesopotamia was made by Sir Leonard Woolley, who excavated the ancient Sumerian city of Ur in 1927. His work was sponsored by a joint effort of the British Museum and the University of Pennsylvania. Woolley's findings greatly advanced our knowledge of everyday life, art, architecture, literature, government and religion in Mesopotamia. Perhaps his most spectacular discovery was that of the royal tombs which date from c. 2700 BC. The tombs revealed the practice of the sacrificial burial of a dead king's servants, musicians, soldiers and the rest of his retinue! They seemed to have drunk voluntarily a cup of poison.

6. Another important discovery made by Woolley was geological evidence of a great flood. He showed that there had been a great flood in the valley of the Tigris and Euphrates rivers that had left an eight-foot-thick layer of silt. What is the significance of this discovery? (AN)

_____

_____

_____

_____

The Mesopotamian Legacy

Libraries: Thousands of clay tablets with copies of older works were found at the palace of Sennacherib and his grandson Ashurbanipal at Ninevah. Included were such diverse works as dictionaries, medical works and stories.

Mathematics: The Sumerians based their arithmetic on the numbers 60 and 10. They understood the use of fractions and square roots.

Law: Legal theory was expressed from early times in collections of legal decisions. The best known of these codes, as they were called, is the Code of Hammurabi.

Engineering: In the third millennium BC the first irrigation canals were built in the Sumerian city of Lagash.

7. For which aspects of modern mathematics should we thank the Babylonians and their number system based on the number 60? (C)

_____

_____

_____

_____

Ancient China

Archaeology by Chinese scholars was at first almost exclusively limited to historical and literary studies; therefore, they ignored artifacts which did not have inscriptions. When Westerners began to organize explorations in the early 1920s, they became interested in objects without inscriptions. The Chinese, too, began to share in this interest, and many important discoveries were made. At Chou-k'ou-tien, one of the first sites to be excavated, was found an artifact estimated to date back about 500,000 years.

Archaeologists have found over 150,000 artifacts with evidence of Chinese writing. Some date back to about 1500 BC. Animal bones and tortoise shells were scratched with signs, 1,400 of which are readable. The signs are in three forms: pictograms, ideograms and phonograms. It was from these pictures that the Chinese symbols, put into a standard index after 213 BC, developed.

1. Make up your own picture signs. Write a message and scratch it on a hard substance. Have a classmate try to decipher your message. (AP, S)

2. Keeping in mind that many different languages are spoken in China, explain the value of Chinese character writing. (C, AN)

_____

_____

_____

_____

3. You have been asked to plan an exhibit of ancient Chinese art for a museum. Assuming you can obtain any artifacts you desire, create a descriptive brochure of the artifacts you will include and the approximate dates they were created. (K, C, AP)

4. The ancient Chinese carefully guarded their secret of how to make silk, their most important trading product. The punishment for breaking the secret was death by torture. It wasn't until the second century AD that the secret method was leaked to Japan via Korea. Make a how-to booklet explaining how silk is made. (K, C, AP)

5. List three uses of silk by the ancient Chinese. (K, C)

_____

_____

_____

_____

_____

The earliest Chinese settled in the North China Plain, along the Yellow River Valley. Although when wet, the thick yellow soil (called loess) was very fertile, the climate of the North China Plain was unpredictable. When it rained too much, there was flooding; when it didn't rain enough, the loess turned to dust. For this reason, nature was extremely important to them. Men who specialized in studying the weather, sky and magic played an important role in their government.

6. All four of the earliest civilized societies had something in common. Keeping in mind the geographic locations of the civilizations of Mesopotamia, Egypt, the Indus Valley and China, tell what outstanding feature they all have in common. (K, C)

_____

_____

_____

_____

7. Make a poster of scientific instruments of ancient China. Include a brief description of each. (K, C, AP)

8. Draw a picture of the Great Wall of China and explain why it was built. (K, C)

_____

_____

_____

_____

_____

Ancient Greece

Greece was a favorite spot for antiquaries. When it was under Turkish rule, not much was done to protect its monuments. For example, the Parthenon, the temple to the goddess Athena at Athens, was used by the Turks as a gunpowder storehouse in the seventeenth century and almost destroyed during a siege.

1. Draw a picture of the Parthenon. (K, AP)

2. Find out what is meant by the "Elgin Marbles." Explain. (K, C)

_____

_____

_____

_____

_____

The Discovery of Troy

Heinrich Schliemann is probably is the most famous archaeologist. Even as a young boy he was fascinated by the history of the ancient Greeks and especially by Homer's epic poem, the *Iliad.* His interest first began when his father, a poor German pastor, gave him a history book with a picture of Troy in flames. That picture stayed with him forever.

Although born of poor parents, Schliemann was very enterprising. By the time he was thirty-six years of age, he had amassed a fortune large enough to retire and devote himself to the archaeology of Greece and Turkey. His primary interest was the identification of the site of Homeric Troy. Many scholars of his time thought Troy was a mere legend. Of those who did believe Homer's words to be based on fact, most thought it had stood on the hill called Bunarbashi. Schliemann argued that Bunarbashi did not fit Homer's descriptions and set out to prove that Hisarlik was the site of ancient Troy.

In 1871 Heinrich Schliemann began to dig at Hisarlik, Turkey. He was the first to dig out a city-mound layer by layer. Believing Homeric Troy would be at the lowest level, he dug through the top layers without much concern.

Schliemann incorrectly assumed that the second city from the bottom was Homer's Troy. He thought that the gold treasure he found was Priam's treasure. Actually, a city closer to the top layer was Homer's Troy. The city that Schliemann thought was Troy was built about 2,000 years before the Trojan War. In fact, it was a prehistoric Bronze Age civilization.

In 1875 Schliemann decided to go to Greece to dig up the grave of King Agamemnon in Mycenae. Unlike Troy, Mycenae contained excavated graves he believed to be of Agamemnon and other Homeric heroes. Once again he was wrong. But once again his find was even more important than what he had sought. He had discovered another prehistoric Bronze Age civilization—a great civilization that built great palaces, wore fine jewels and made beautiful gold and silver objects.

Schliemann's contributions to archaeology were tremendous. He proved that a great civilization, previously unknown to scholars, existed in the second millennium before Christ. With Schliemann's discoveries, historians could add two prehistoric Bronze Age civilizations.

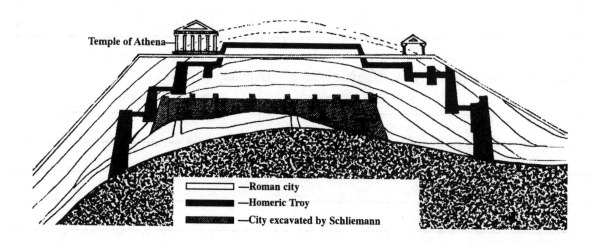

Temple of Athena

☐ —Roman city
■ —Homeric Troy
▨ —City excavated by Schliemann

1. On another sheet of paper draw a map and locate the site of ancient Troy. (K, AP)

2. The site at Hisarlik revealed nine layers. In the bottom layer were pottery and ivory objects, but there were no bronze artifacts. Keeping in mind this fact and also the civilizations then known to historians, explain why Schliemann, in his haste, concluded that the second layer from the bottom was Homeric Troy. (C, AN)

_____

_____

_____

_____

3. Homer's *Iliad* inspired Heinrich Schliemann to find Homeric Troy. It describes an apparently real war between the Greeks and the Trojans; however, the cause of the war was obviously legend. Research the legendary cause of the Trojan War. Draw a series of pictures to illustrate the legend. (Add more boxes if needed.) (C, AP)

4. Schliemann's discoveries have often been compared to those of Christopher Columbus. Do you think this comparison is valid? Why or why not? (C, AN, E)

_____

_____

_____

_____

5. Prepare a question-and-answer session between Helen of Troy and her psychiatrist, who is trying to rid Helen of her guilt. If you wish, work with a classmate. One of you will play the role of Helen, and the other will play the role of her psychiatrist. Then switch roles. (AN, S)

6. Some modern archaeologists have criticized Heinrich Schliemann's methods of excavation. When he dug at Hisarlik, the trench he drove into the hill removed half of it. Having little interest in post-Homeric times and believing Homeric Troy to be near the bottom, he destroyed much of the top layers. Keeping in mind that his work was done in the 1870s and 1880s, evaluate his work. (AN, E)

_____

_____

_____

_____

_____

_____

Ancient Rome: Pompeii and Herculaneum

Although not completely recovered from a very destructive earthquake that had occurred in AD 62, by AD 79 life in Pompeii and Herculaneum was very pleasant. Pompeii was a bustling port town with an amphitheater, public baths, taverns, a variety of shops and other conveniences. Many of Pompeii's citizens were wealthy and they rode the streets in their horse-drawn chariots. Herculaneum was more quiet and secluded, but its citizens also enjoyed their lives.

In early August 79, tremors were felt in the two towns, but they were not strong enough to cause concern. Then suddenly, on the morning of August 24, the earth began to shake violently. The tremors were followed by a terrifying explosion. Mt. Vesuvius had erupted.

A dense black cloud rose high into the sky. Great pieces of rock were hurled into the air and came crashing down onto Pompeii. Showers of ash and lapilli covered the town. Those who fled immediately managed to escape; the others were buried alive. Even those who escaped into the countryside, however, were not safe. Many later died from the poisonous sulfur fumes that had formed.

Those who had escaped unharmed returned to Pompeii a few days later with the hope of salvaging some of their belongings. But when they arrived, they found that the city was almost completely buried under the soft ash and lapilli. Little could be saved.

Herculaneum was even closer to Mt. Vesuvius than was Pompeii. The citizens fled as soon as they saw the flow of viscous material approaching. The mud-like material poured through the doors and windows and completely filled the buildings and streets. What's more, unlike the soft material that covered Pompeii, the volcanic materials that covered Herculaneum was a type that hardens upon cooling.

In spite of the fact that records of the disaster existed and the fact that the names of the towns appeared on maps, Pompeii and Herculaneum were eventually forgotten. As centuries passed, soil gradually formed over the debris. The soil was fertile and people once again settled there to cultivate the land.

Once in a while people's interest in Pompeii and Herculaneum was sparked. The eyewitness account of Pliny the Younger, as written to the historian Tacitus, was read with excitement when published. There was also much talk when fragments of marble and coins bearing the inscription of Emperor Nero were found in the sixteenth century. But no one was inspired enough to begin excavation.

It was in 1709 that excavation of the buried cities first began in Herculaneum. Austria had occupied southern Italy. A worker hired by an Austrian officer, the Compte d'Elbeuf, had found three beautiful marble statues near the foot of Mt. Vesuvius. Eventually, those statues came into the possession of Augustus III of Poland. When the daughter of Augustus, Maria-Amalia, became the wife of Charles III of Naples (later Charles III of Spain), she wanted more statues to decorate her gardens. Charles ordered excavation to begin at Herculaneum in 1738.

Other excavations were carried out from time to time. But, like Charles, the excavators were more interested in collecting treasures than in understanding the past. Digging, for the most part, was haphazard and irresponsible.

The haphazard digging ended in 1860 when the Italian archaeologist Guiseppe Fiorelli became director of the excavations. He divided Pompeii into nine regions; he then numbered the insulae, or blocks, and the houses within the insulae. Fiorelli also developed the technique of making casts of bodies by pouring cement into the hollows formed in the volcanic ash when the bodies disintegrated. Intensive excavation was once again carried on in Pompeii from 1924–1961 by Amadeo Maiuri. By 1970 about three-fourths of the town was excavated.

The results were amazing, for the volcanic material that destroyed the city also preserved what was in it. When the excavation was complete, the archaeologists saw before them life as it was almost 2,000 years earlier. Even the food that the people were about to eat could be seen. And the paintings on the walls appeared in color as brilliant as if they had just been completed.

The work at Herculaneum was more difficult not only because of the hardness of the fill, but also because the modern town of Resina had been built on the site. Still, the finds there were also remarkable.

Pompeii

The artifacts found at Herculaneum and Pompeii had a tremendous influence upon European culture, but that is not where their real importance lies. The remains of these two sites were in such a remarkable state of preservation that they provided a wealth of information about the social, economic, political and religious life of the ancient Greco-Roman world.

1. Draw a map that includes the following sites: Naples, Pompeii, Herculaneum and Mt. Vesuvius. (K)

2. Why was it strange that Pompeii and Herculaneum were forgotten? (C)

_____

_____

_____

3. Make a diorama of a typical villa for a wealthy citizen after the earthquake of AD 62. (C, AP, S)

4. Before the earthquake of 62 many of the houses, temples and other buildings in Pompeii and Herculaneum were still in the Greek style. When the Roman Senate supervised the reconstruction, they had the architects design all of the buildings in the Roman style. (Some scholars even believe that they deliberately destroyed some Greek-styled buildings that survived the quake!) Analyze their reasons for doing so. (AN)

_____

_____

_____

_____

5. Shrines were found in many of the private homes in Pompeii. What does this tell us about the people? (AN)

_____

_____

_____

_____

_____

6. Write an original myth to explain the eruption of Mt. Vesuvius. Illustrate your myth. (S)

_____

_____

_____

_____

_____

_____

_____

_____

_____

_____

_____

_____

_____

_____

_____

_____

_____

_____

The Minoans

The Bronze Age civilization of Crete is known as the Minoan civilization. It is named after King Minos, the legendary ruler of Crete, although it is not clear whether or not there actually was such a ruler. The civilization is divided into three periods: Early Minoan (*c.* 3000–2100 BC), Middle Minoan (*c.* 2100–1550 BC) and Late Minoan (*c.* 1550–1100 BC). Its capital was at Knossos.

The person responsible for excavation of the palace at Knossos was Sir Arthur Evans. Although he himself was not an expert archaeologist, his assistant Duncan Mackenzie *was.* Evans also hired professional architects to remain with him throughout so that he could accurately describe and restore the ruins. What they uncovered must be ranked among the most important archaeological finds of Mediterranean antiquity, for what they found was the oldest European civilization!

The palace itself served not only as a royal residence, but also housed a great number of civil servants. There were a tremendous number of rooms. Among them were several rooms in which to press oil and others in which to store it, for the king's wealth had come from olive oil. There were a number of conveniences that are not even found in some parts of the world today: drains, lavatories, ventilators and more!

A lot was learned from the frescoes and reliefs that decorated the walls. Many portrayed a dangerous sport which involved athletes leaping over bulls. The bull was also used as a design on seals and vases. Along with the labrys, or double-sided ax, it was the most important symbol.

Evans worked at Knossos for a quarter of a century. His work was so detailed and precise that even if Crete were completely destroyed, archaeologists would still have a picture of Knossos and the magnificent palace of the legendary King Minos.

1. Make a time line and mark the periods of Minoan civilization. (C, AP)

2. Read the legend of King Minos and the Minotaur. Draw a series of pictures to illustrate the legend. (C, AP)

3. Describe the palace Evans found at Knossos. How can it explain the legend of the Labyrinth? (K, C, AP, AN)

_____

_____

_____

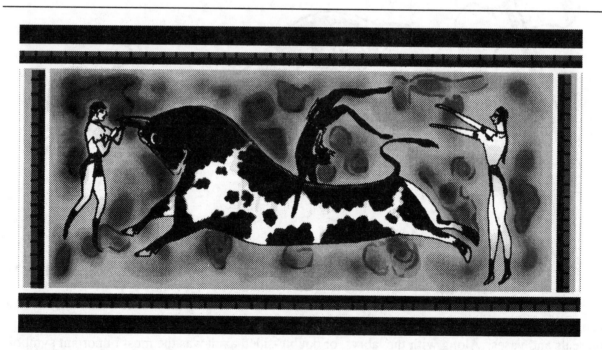

4. The bull-vaulting sport seems to have involved an acrobat who seized a charging bull by its horns and vaulted over its head; he then did a handspring from the bull's back while a female assistant steadied the bull by holding its horns. (Some believe the activities occurred in the opposite order.) Paint in the Minoan style a fresco of this bull-vaulting event. (C, AP, S)

5. What Sir Arthur Evans found at Knossos was one layer of ruins that appeared to be several different palaces. Each group of builders, however, seemed to keep what they could of the old structure and to add on to that structure. They only destroyed what was necessary. Compare and contrast this set of circumstances with what Heinrich Schliemann found at Troy. Also, what does the fact that it was in one layer tell us about the length of time Knossos was occupied? (C, AN)

_____

_____

_____

_____

_____

6. Research Minoan pottery. Make a vase in the Minoan style. (C, AP, AN)

7. Sir Arthur Evans has been criticized by some archaeologists for reconstructing the ruins. Critics were especially disturbed by such practices as replacing missing wooden pillars with concrete ones and for strengthening ancient masonry with steel girders. Yet the palace later withstood severe earthquake shocks that devastated nearby areas. Judge the decision made by Evans to reconstruct the palace and to use materials not used in the original construction. (E)

_____

_____

_____

_____

_____

Stonehenge

Stonehenge, located on the Salisbury Plain in England, is one of the best known monuments of the ancient world. It is a large circular setting of large standing stones and comprises an area 320 feet in diameter. Around the stones is a low bank and around it a broken shallow ditch or moat. Inside the bank are two shallow circular ditches called the North Barrow and the South Barrow; however, they are not actually barrows, or prehistoric grave mounds. Also as part of the plan are a number of holes which had been dug up and later filled up with soil and debris.

There are two different kinds of stones. The very large stones are called sarsens. Medieval Englishmen called them "Sarsen stones" because they believed that the Saracens, their term for foreign nonbelievers, had created them. The sarsens are made out of sandstone, which can be found about twenty miles north of Stonehenge. The smaller stones are made or dolerite and rhylite, igneous rocks called bluestones because of their bluish color. The fascinating thing is that these rocks have been proved to have come from an area in Wales about 135 miles from Stonehenge. The sea and land route they would have taken would have made the journey about 240 miles.

Stonehenge was built in three phases: Stonehenge I (*c*. 1800 BC), Stonehenge II (probably seventeenth century BC) and Stonehenge III (*c*. 1600 BC). Although other circular structures exist, the sarsen structure of Stonehenge is unique in Europe. The stones were placed in four main groups. On the outside was a circle of sarsens, at one time consisting of thirty upright stones ranging from about 25 to 35 tons each and topped with seven-ton lintels (horizontal beams) to form a closed circle; next came a circle of sixty undressed bluestones; then came a horseshoe of sarsens, consisting of five trilithons, or sets of three stones (two 45-ton uprights capped by a large lintel); and the inner group was a horseshoe of smoothed bluestones. There were also several miscellaneous stones.

Some who studied the monument believed it was connected with the Druids. The Druids were Celtic priests who ruled much of Europe. They came to Britain from Gaul in the fourth century BC. Today most archaeologists believe that the Druids did not build Stonehenge, although some agree that they might have worshiped there.

Stonehenge probably was built as a place of worship; however, the nature of the religion that was practiced there is still not known. Some believe that it was a temple for sky worship. Perhaps they are correct, but as of now at least, there is not enough evidence to be certain.

1. Draw a diagram of Stonehenge. (C, AP)

2. Why didn't Stonehenge have to be "discovered" like most of the artifacts studied by archaeologists? (C)

_____

_____

_____

3. Show on a time line the various stages in which Stonehenge was built. (K)

4. Early work on Stonehenge was done by antiquaries. Compare and contrast an antiquary and an archaeologist. (C, AN)

_____

_____

_____

_____

_____

5. According to an old legend, Merlin, the Wizard of King Arthur's court, brought Stonehenge bodily from Ireland by magic. Write your own fantasy about the creation of Stonehenge. (S)

6. In the 1950s Professors Atkinson, Piggott and Stone investigated Stonehenge. Their work resulted in the radiocarbon dating of the Aubrey Holes (named after John Aubrey who discovered them in the seventeenth century) and the discovery of most of the details from which the history of Stonehenge has been pieced together. The three men, however, dug only in half of the area covered by the monument. They left the other half alone for future archaeologists. Evaluate this decision. (E)

_____

_____

_____

_____

_____

_____

_____

Earliest Americans

Evidence shows that humans have probably lived in the Americas for more than 15,000 years. They came from Asia, across what is now the Bering Strait, at a time when glacial ice had lowered the level of the sea. Even in early times lifestyles varied among these native Americans. The earliest major culture type was the Big Game Hunter. But even as that culture still flourished, a different culture developed in the Southwest—a desert culture. The farming culture of the Americas probably began in Mexico about 7000 BC.

The Anasazi

When archaeologists excavated the arid lands of the Mesa Verde region of the Southwest, where the Anasazi had dwelled, they found an interesting situation. The top several layers of occupation contained pottery and potsherds as expected, but the lower strata contained no potsherds; instead they contained baskets, sandals and other woven artifacts. The strata are now usually classified into these developmental periods: Basket-Maker Period (AD 100–500); Modified Basket-Maker Period (500–700); Developmental Pueblo Period (700–1050); Classic Pueblo (1050–1300); Regressive Pueblo (1300–1700); and Modern Pueblo (1700 to date).

Archaeologists do not know where the Basket Makers originated. They do know from the fine craftsmanship of the artifacts found in the earliest strata that they were already excellent basket weavers when they arrived. They also know that they had learned to supplement their diet of wild seeds they gathered by cultivating maize and pumpkins.

1. Archaeologists assume that before the Anasazi settled into the more permanent pit houses of the Modified Basket Maker Period, they were nomadic hunters and gatherers who took refuge in the caves and crude brush shelters. Analyze the reasons for this conclusion. (AN)

_____

_____

_____

_____

_____

_____

_____

_____

_____

As agriculture became more important, pottery was introduced and more permanent pit-house villages began to appear. Eventually, as extended families pooled their resources, large pueblo villages were formed in the mesa tops. Stone masonry began to replace pole-and-mud construction. The pit houses became ceremonial chambers, called kivas. Finally, the population increased to the point where the people had to move from the mesa tops. It was during the Classic Pueblo Period that the great cliff houses and large, apartment-like structures were built along the canyon and mesa walls.

2. Paint a mural of a cliff house of the Classic Pueblo Period. (C, AP)

The Classic Period came to an end when the people suddenly abandoned their cliff houses and large community houses. In a great mass movement, they headed south and mingled with the other desert dwellers. It was the Anasazi who became the ancestors of the modern Pueblo Indians.

3. *Anasazi* is a Navajo name. Find out what it means. (K)

_____

4. No one is certain why the Anasazi abandoned their great cliff houses and community dwellings. Research the possible causes for such a move. (C, AN)

_____

_____

_____

_____

_____

Many of the elements of the Anasazi culture came from their neighbors of Old Mexico, the Maya and the Aztecs.

The Maya

The Mayan civilization of southern Mexico and Central America was the most brilliant pre-Columbian civilization ever discovered. It flourished from the third century to the sixteenth century, when the Spaniards arrived.

An American by the name of John Lloyd Stephens had read about ancient Indian ruins in the jungles of Central America and in the Yucatán. In 1839 he decided to go to Central America to find and study the ruins. He asked his English artist friend, Frederick Catherwood, to join him.

After an extremely treacherous journey, they arrived in the village of Copán, in Honduras. It was said that the ruins there were well preserved. At last their native guide led them to a pyramid and other monuments even more wonderful than they had hoped.

Stephens explored while Catherwood made careful and detailed drawings of the sculptured stones that covered the stairways, walls and monuments. When Stephens and Catherwood questioned their guide about who had built the abandoned city, the guide could not tell them. No one knew. From Copán, they went to other forgotten cities.

When Stephens published his book two years later, it caused a great sensation. He and Catherwood had put an end to the theory that only savages had lived in America. The people who were responsible for these artifacts were wonderful artists and architects.

The work of Stephens and Catherwood inspired other archaeologists and scholars to study the area. They learned that a brilliant people called the Maya had built the abandoned cities. The Maya had invented a hieroglyphic form of writing and two kinds of numbers (similar to the way that we use both Arabic and Roman numerals.) They also had invented a sign for zero, which Europeans didn't have until it was brought from India in the eighth century!) What's more, they had worked out a nearly perfect calendar!

The archaeologists also learned something strange. Every twenty years (more often in the large cities) the Maya set up new pyramids, palaces and other monuments. This went on for about 500 to 600 years. Then suddenly it all stopped. Copán erected its final monument in 800. Tikal, the largest Mayan city, built its last monument by 869. Although archaeologists have tried to guess what caused the abandonment, no one can be sure.

1. Draw a picture of the principal crop of the Maya. (K)

2. The rain god Chac seems to have been more important in the Yucatán than in the southern regions of Mayan civilization. Why? (C, AN)

3. Make a model of a Mayan pyramid. (K, C, AP)

4. Archaeological remains such as temples, tombs, sculpture and pottery provided a wealth of information regarding the Mayan religion. Research and write a report on Mayan religion during the Classic Period. (K, C, AP, AN)

5. The Mayans wrote records of their history in books known to us as "codices." They contained an elaborately detailed, brightly colored picture writing and were painted on leather or on paper made from the fiber of a native tree. Make up your own hieroglyphs and paint a codex imitating the Mayan style. (C, AP ,S)

6. The Mayan codices would have provided a great deal of information; however, the Spanish priests had them destroyed. Only four known codices remain. Judge the destruction of these native books by the Spaniards. (AN, E)

The Aztec Calendar Stone

The Aztecs, who ruled a large empire in the fifteenth and sixteenth centuries in what is now central and southern Mexico, were much more barbarous than the Maya. They believed that they were the people of the Sun and that the sun god had to be nourished in order to survive. For that reason, human sacrifice became an important part of the Aztec religion.

1. The Aztec calendar was not as accurate as that of the Maya, but like most of the Central American societies, the Aztecs were deeply interested in time. Although the above stone sculpture is known as the Aztec Calendar Stone, it is actually something else. Keeping in mind the most important aspect of the Aztec religion, can you guess what this monument really was. (C, AN)

_____

_____

_____

_____

_____

_____

The Inca

When the Spaniards arrived in South America in 1532, they found a civilization of native American people called the Inca. The Incan Empire included what is now Peru, Bolivia, Ecuador and part of Brazil. Their capital had been established at Cuzco in the twelfth century. In the early fifteenth century they began to conquer other peoples, and by the time the Spaniards arrived at the scene, the Inca controlled about twelve million people speaking at least twenty different languages. Once conquered, however, these people were accepted into their society and treated as any other Inca.

The Inca's economy depended upon agriculture and, like their ancestors, they terraced the steep slopes of the mountains and cultivated a variety of crops: maize (corn), white and sweet potatoes, squash, tomatoes, peanuts, cocoa and more. Technology was also advanced. Palaces, temples and fortifications were built. They also had a fine system of roads, which ran from Cuzco to all parts of the Empire.

The society was highly stratified. The first great emperor was called Inca. His name was Manqo Qhapaq (Manco Capac in Spanish). The emperor and his aristocratic bureaucracy ruled with a strong hand. Land was owned collectively, each peasant being allotted an amount deemed appropriate by the rulers. In spite of strict rule, however, the emperor was comparatively fair, and the people were probably not unhappy.

The Incan religion was based upon the belief in a sun god. Although the conquered were allowed to maintain their own religious practices, they had to accept the religion of the sun god, too.

When the Spaniards came, the Incan Empire was brought to an end; however, traces of their language and customs still survive in their descendants living in the Andes of South America.

The ancient fortress of Machu Picchu is located about fifty miles from Cuzco, Peru. It is the most complete model ever found of what an Incan city looked like and is one of the few pre-Columbian urban centers found almost unchanged; nevertheless, because of its location, it went undetected by the Spaniards. The "lost city" of Machu Picchu was discovered by Hiram Bingham of Yale University in 1911. It's hard to imagine how such a site could be "lost" for nearly 500 years!

1. Draw a map which shows the extent of the Incan Empire at its peak. Show the location of Cuzco. (K, AP)

2. Find out the location of Machu Picchu and explain why it went undiscovered by the Spaniards. (K, C)

_____

_____

_____

_____

3. Paint a picture of Machu Picchu. (C, AP)

4. The Mochica were a pre-Inca people. Little is known about them except for their exquisitely decorated jugs and bowls and beautifully embroidered mantles. The Mochica decorated their jugs with detailed paintings of their daily lives. Out of clay, make a jug or bowl. Decorate it with scenes from your daily life so that if found hundreds of years from now, future archaeologists could use it to learn what life in your society was like. (C, AP, AN, S, E)

Accidental Finds

Chance often plays an important role in archaeological discoveries.

Cave Paintings

In the woods near Lascaux, France, as four boys looked for their dog that had strayed, they came across an underground cave. The cave they discovered turned out to be one used during the Old Stone Age. Archaeologists estimated the paintings on the cave wall to be over 15,000 years old!

Other prehistoric caves were similarly found in Altamira, Spain.

The Dead Sea Scrolls

One of the most important accidental finds was that of the Dead Sea Scrolls in 1947.

A young Bedouin shepherd was searching for his stray goat along the shores of the Dead Sea in Jordan. While looking in a cave, he and his friends found rows of clay jars containing rolls of leather and papyrus. The rolls were wrapped in linen. Among the scrolls, now known as the Dead Sea Scrolls, was the whole book of Isaiah in Hebrew. It appears to date from the first century before Christ, which made it about 1,000 years older than any previously-found manuscript of the Hebrew Old Testament.

1. Locate on a map the area in which the Dead Sea Scrolls were found. (K)

2. In what occupations or vocations might people be likely to unearth an archaeological find by chance? On a separate sheet, draw a picture to illustrate one of your ideas. (C, AP, AN)

_____

_____

_____

_____

_____

3. Make a large mural which represents a prehistoric cave painting. Draw a sketch of your idea here. (C, AP, S)

4. Why, do you think, did prehistoric people bother to create paintings on the walls and ceilings of dark caves even though they could hardly be seen? (C, AN)

_____

_____

_____

_____

_____

5. Write an original story in which your main character accidentally makes a shocking archaeological find. On the lines below write a summary of the plot. Then draw a picture illustrating your story. (S)

_____

_____

_____

_____

_____

_____

6. Studying the Old Testament for historical evidence presents several problems. Scholars make a critical study of it on two levels: "higher" and "lower" criticism. It is easy to understand why higher criticism is difficult. Higher criticism involves such aspects as who wrote the passages, when the passages were written, and what were the author's sources of information. Lower criticism involves deciphering the text—deciding exactly what the ancient writer meant. Keeping in mind the means by which the manuscripts were written, tell what problems may arise for the "lower" critic. (C, AN, E)

_____

_____

_____

_____

Underwater Archaeology

Underwater archaeology is relatively new. Although it involves the same basic techniques as land archaeology—observation, discovery and recording—there are, of course, major differences. For one thing, an underwater archaeologist would be at quite a disadvantage if he or she were not a trained diver.

1. French scientist Jacques-Yves Cousteau developed the breathing apparatus known as the scuba. The most commonly used form is the aqualung. Evaluate the importance of this invention to underwater archaeology. (C, AN, E)

_____

_____

_____

_____

2. The word *scuba* is actually an acronym. Try to guess the words that make up the acronym. Then check in a dictionary to see if you were correct. (C, AP)

S _____

C _____

U _____

B _____

A _____

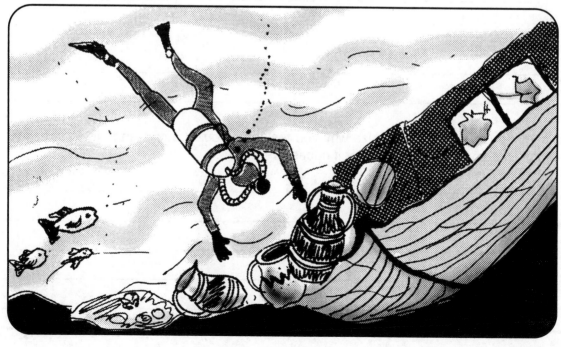

Take Me Along

Fill out this application as a volunteer to join an archaeological expedition. Think about the necessary personality and educational qualifications. (K, C, AP, AN, E)

APPLICATION TO ASSIST ON AN
ARCHAEOLOGICAL DIG IN _____

Name: _____ Date: _____

Type of Job Desired:

_____

Personal Qualifications:

_____

_____

Educational Qualifications:

_____

_____

Character References (at least four):

_____   _____

_____   _____

Related Experience:

_____

_____

In 75 words or less, summarize why you feel you should be chosen to join the expedition. Use another sheet of paper if necessary.

_____

_____

_____

_____

_____

Just for Fun!

1. WHAT A SITE!
Decide upon a site. Make a list of artifacts that might be found there. Be original! Exchange lists with your classmates and try to guess what type of site is being discussed. (C, AP, S)

2. WHO'S WHO IN ARCHAEOLOGY
Create a "Who's Who in Archaeology" booklet. Include people who have made important contributions to the field of archaeology. Illustrate your booklet with appropriate drawings. (K, C, AP, S, E)

3. IN THE LAND OF _____
Write a short science-fiction story in which your main character is transported back in time to an ancient land. (C, AP, S)

4. GARBAGE GOSSIP
Make a list of the garbage you threw away last week. What could future archaeologists learn about the way you live from your garbage? (AN, E)

5. STAMP OF HONOR
Design a postage stamp to honor a man or woman whom you feel made a great contribution to the field of archaeology. (C, E)

6. HOW TIME FLIES
Make a time line that shows when at least five important ancient civilizations flourished. (K, AP)

7. COMPARE AND CONTRAST
Compare and contrast two major ancient civilizations. (C, AN)

8. SCHOOL YARD ARTIFACTS
Make a list of artifacts that might be found at the site of your school one thousand years from now. Draw a picture of the artifacts. (C, AP)

9. PIECING IT TOGETHER

On heavy paper make a detailed painting or drawing of an artifact. Cut it into pieces and have a friend try to piece together your "artifact." (C, AP)

10. DETAILS COUNT!

Choose an everyday object. Pretend that it is one thousand years from now and that you are seeing the artifact for the first time. Make up a detailed card describing it. (C, AP)

11. CULTURE

Re-read the explanation of what is meant by culture. Write a report describing your own culture. (C, AP, AN)

12. COURSE OF STUDY

Write to several colleges. Find out what courses are recommended for a planned career as an archaeologist. Prepare a suggested course of study. (K, C, AP)

13. A MOSAIC

Cut colored construction paper into tiny pieces. Make a mosaic in the style of the ancient Romans. (K, C, AP, S)

14. RIDDLES

Make up a series of riddles about ancient cultures. (K, C, AP, AN, S)

Pre-Test

Circle the correct answer for each.

1. The systematic recovery and study of material evidence of past cultures is _____.

   A. Sociology   B. Archaeology   C. Anthropology   D. Geology

2. Objects shaped by human workmanship are _____.

   A. Artifacts   B. Fossils   C. Antiques   D. Cultures

3. Another word for chronology is _____.

   A. Dating   B. Illness   C. Culture   D. Archaeology

4. The wedge-shaped writing of the Sumerians is called _____.

   A. Hieroglyphics   B. Ziggurat   C. Cuneiform   D. Cartouche

5. The pictorial-symbol writing of the ancient Egyptians is called _____.

   A. Hieroglyphics   B. Ziggurat   C. Cuneiform   D. Cartouche

6. The behavior, art, beliefs and institutions characteristic of a community is its _____.

   A. Chronology   B. Culture   C. Tell   D. Antiquities

7. The word used to describe the era before recorded history is _____.

   A. Prehistoric   B. Ancient   C. Hieroglyphic   D. Archaeology

8. The pyramids were actually _____.

   A. Storehouses   B. Government buildings   C. Theaters   D. Tombs

9. We call the earliest period of human culture the Stone Age because of the _____.

   A. Tools   B. Homes   C. Beliefs   D. Religion

10. Howard Carter discovered the tomb of this pharaoh.

    A. Ramseses   B. Tutankhamen   C. Thutmose   D. Ptolemy

Introduction to Archaeology

Fill in the blanks.

1. _____ is the systematic retrieval and study of material evidence of humans' past.

2. Objects produced by human workmanship are called _____.

3. The knowledge, beliefs, art and institutions of a society make up its _____.

4. A tell is a type of _____.

5. The method of digging out a site layer by layer is called _____.

6. When a site has been excavated and the strata identified, the _____ level will usually be the oldest; the _____ level will usually be the most recent.

7. The pattern of horizontal and vertical lines which form uniform squares often used in excavation is a _____.

8. Three tools used by archaeologists are _____, _____ and _____.

9. "In situ" refers to _____ the artifact was found.

10. Fragments of pottery are called _____.

The Ages of Human Existence

Fill in the blanks.

1. The ages of human existence are based upon the _____ that were made.

2. We refer to the time before written history as _____.

3. _____ is the name for the Old Stone Age.

4. _____ is the name for the New Stone Age.

5. In most places civilization was accompanied by two inventions: _____ and _____.

6. The first two ages of civilization were the _____ Age and the _____ Age.

7. Another word for chronology is _____.

8. _____ is the counting of the rings of trees to date past events.

9. In Scandinavia dating is sometimes based on the number of layers of sediment, called _____.

10. The radioactive form of the element _____ is helpful in dating artifacts.

Ancient Egypt

Fill in the blanks.

1. To preserve bodies, Egyptians practiced a system called _____.

2. The pyramids were actually magnificent _____.

3. British archaeologist _____ began his work in Egypt in 1880; he is credited with developing a systematic method of excavation.

4. The study of the _____ led to the decipherment of Egyptian hieroglyphics; it was largely the work of Thomas Young and _____.

5. The Egyptians learned to make a paperlike material called _____.

6. Howard Carter discovered the tomb of _____, sometimes called the boy king.

7. The area in which Carter made his discovery is called the _____.

8. The Egyptian monument called the _____ had the head of a man and the body of a lion.

9. Egyptian civilization was said to be a gift of the _____ River.

10. Artifacts were well preserved in Egypt because of its _____ climate.

Mesopotamia

Fill in the blanks.

1. Mesopotamia means "Land Between the Rivers." The rivers it refers to are the
   _____ and the _____.

2. The oldest civilization of Mesopotamia, and probably of the world, was _____.

3. The most important material in Mesopotamia was _____, especially in
   terms of art and literature.

4. The name we give to Mesopotamian writing is _____.

5. The Rosetta Stone had a triple inscription that led to the decipherment of Egyptian hieroglyphics. The _____ had a triple inscription that led to the decipherment of
   cuneiform.

6. The world *cuneiform* means _____.

7. _____ discovered the palace of the Assyrian King Sargon II.

8. A _____ is a staged tower built by the ancient Assyrians and Babylonians.

9. Sir Austen Layard found Ninevah and uncovered the palace of _____,
   where many cuneiform tablets from the state archives were found.

10. Sir Leonard Woolley excavated the ancient Sumerian city of _____, where
    he found royal tombs from *c.* 2700 BC with evidence of sacrificial burials.

Ancient China

Fill in the blanks.

1. Early Chinese archaeological scholars were interested in artifacts with _____.

2. Chinese writing dates back to *c.* 1500 BC. Evidence of this fact comes from more than 150,000 _____ and _____, which had been scratched with signs.

3. The ancient Chinese guarded their secret for making _____, their most important product for trade.

4. The ancient Chinese civilization began in the valley of the _____.

5. The _____, about 1,500 miles (2,415 km) long, formed a solid barrier of defense between China and her northern neighbors.

The Ancient Greco-Roman World

Fill in the blanks.

1. The word _____ is used to describe a collector of antiquities.

2. The _____ was the name of the temple to the goddess Athena in Athens.

3. _____ discovered the site of ancient Troy.

4. The civilization that Schliemann believed to be Troy and Mycenae of Homeric times were actually two _____ Age civilizations.

5. The Bronze Age civilization of Crete is known as the _____ Civilization.

6. _____ was responsible for the excavation of the palace at Knossos.

7. According to legend, King Minos kept the creature known as the _____ in the Labyrinth.

8. The total destruction at Pompeii and Herculaneum was due to the eruption of _____.

9. The artifacts found at Pompeii and Herculaneum were in a(n) _____ state of preservation.

10. Although many buildings were in the Greek style before the disaster, they were rebuilt in the _____ style.

Stonehenge

Fill in the blanks.

1. Stonehenge is located on the Salisbury Plain in _____.

2. The very large stones are called _____ because in medieval times it was believed that Saracens erected them.

3. Stonehenge was built in _____ phases.

4. In the past, some scholars believed that Celtic priests, called _____, were connected with Stonehenge.

5. Stonehenge was probably built as a place of _____.

Earliest Americans

Fill in the blanks.

1. *Anasazi* is the name given to the ancient desert dwellers by the _____.

2. When archaeologists excavated the sites where the Anasazi dwelled, they found no potsherds in the lowest levels. Instead they found _____.

3. During the classic period the Anasazi built great _____.

4. The _____ civilization was a great pre-Columbian civilization of southern Mexico and Central America.

5. _____ and his artist friend Frederick Catherwood explored the ancient Native American ruins of Central America.

6. Mayan histories in the form of brightly colored picture writing, called _____, were destroyed by the Spaniards.

7. The Aztec Calendar Stone was actually a monument to the _____.

8. When the Spaniards arrived in South America in 1532, they found a great civilization of native peoples called the _____.

9. _____ is the name of the ancient fortress city about fifty miles from Cuzco, Peru. Because it went unnoticed by the Spaniards and was not re-discovered until 1911, it is sometimes called the Lost City.

10. _____ discovered the Lost City in 1911.

Odds 'n Ends

Fill in the blanks.

1. Important archeological discoveries are often made by chance. Examples of this are the
_____ discovered in Lascaux, France, and in Altamira, Spain.

2. An important find was made by a Bedouin shepherd searching for his stray goat. We call the
artifact he found the _____.

3. _____ invented the aqualung, an important aid to underwater archaeology.

4. The basic techniques of archaeology are _____, _____,
and _____.

5. An underwater archaeologist must also be a skilled _____.

Post-Test

Circle the correct answer for each.

1. A ziggurat could be found in _____.
    A. Egypt   B. Greece   C. Mesopotamia   D. Rome

2. The Paleolithic Age is another term for the _____.
    A. New Stone Age   B. Iron Age   C. Bronze Age   D. Old Stone Age

3. Egypt's artifacts were well preserved because of the _____.
    A. High humidity   B. Dry climate   C. Nile River   D. Workmanship

4. A potsherd is a_____.
    A. Fragment of pottery   B. Storage jar   C. Painted jar   D. Shepherd

5. This was the key to the decipherment of Egyptian hieroglyphics.
    A. Parthenon   B. Rosetta Stone   C. Stonehenge   D. Behistun Rock

6. This city was destroyed by an eruption of Mt. Vesuvius.
    A. Rome   B. Machu Picchu   C. Sumer   D. Pompeii

7. Carbon-14 is useful in _____ a find.
    A. Preserving   B. Deciphering   C. Dating   D. Unearthing

8. A prehistoric monument of upright stones in England is _____.
    A. Stonehenge   B. Machu Picchu   C. Labyrinth   D. Parthenon

9. This man discovered Troy.
A. Howard Carter   B. Leonard Woolley   C. Arthur Evans   D. Heinrich Schliemann

10. Along with the Egyptians, they are believed to have established one of the earliest historic civilizations.
    A. Greeks   B. Sumerians   C. Romans   D. Persians

Archaeology Word Search

```
                    A B
                   T E L L
                  C E L I N D
                 G E D N U O M F
                P K M E G Y P T H J
               D N I F N O Q C A V E
              Z W V L I U N I U R T G A
             X I Y S A E B O P N C S D R E
            A F G H D I L J I L E O N M T Q P
           R F Y G D R Z D A T W I S A U I E S A
          C G G A U E E A W K A Y F N I V F P G G L
         H K O I G R B H F O D Z X O E R T A F R N H E
        A L L C D D A E S B R B I G R H E I C J K J E I O
       E M O J I H M T X T W K C L V M U M T T T K S L H M L
      O O N Z M X A B A C O C D F I E R G U S R Q O L I M E N I
     L P O N A D W A Y C Y P Z A Z V T S I S O R P D K J L K N O T
    O R R G R F T I G R I S A M B D I G D H Y G R A V E S N E N O S H
   G S H A Y J E X C A V A T I O N L C U H I E R O G L Y P H O B P T R I
  Y T C U P X V M E S O P O T A M I A P C I R O T S I H E R P P L O M S Q C
```

ARCHEOLOGY	FIND	POTSHERDS
ARTIFACT	GRAVES	PREHISTORIC
CAVE	HIEROGLYPH	PYRAMID
CHRONOLOGY	MAYA	STONEHENGE
CIVILIZATION	MESOPOTAMIA	SUMERIANS
CUNEIFORM	MOUND	TELL
DIG	NILE	TIGRIS
EGYPT	OBELISK	TROY
EXCAVATION	PALEOLITHIC	ZIGGURAT
FIELDWORK		

Archaeology Crossword Puzzle

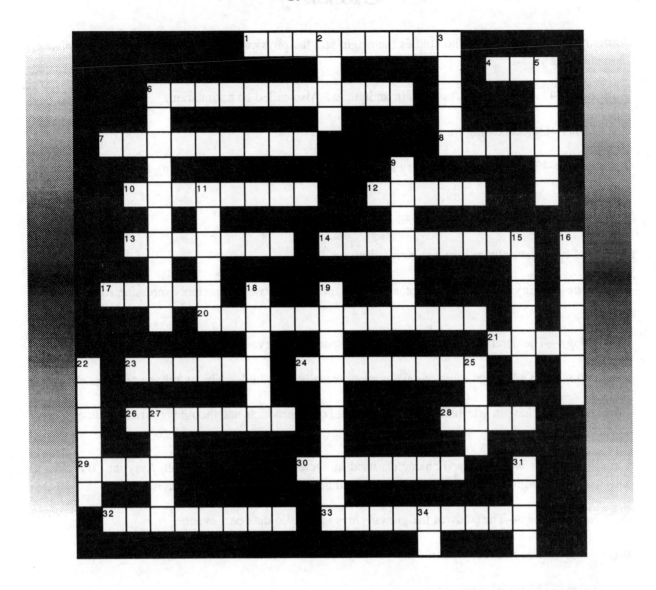

Across

1. Oval around hieroglyphs representing royalty.
4. An archaeological excavation.
6. Adjective describing something before recorded history.
7. Examination of a site before excavation.
8. One of the very large stones at Stonehenge.
10. Terraced temple tower of the Assyrians and the Babylonians.
12. Trowel, brushes, and sieve are some used by archaeologists.
13. A layer of the earth.
14. Written in wedge-shaped characters.
17. A layer of sediment in a glacial lake.
20. The study of layers of earth.
21. Ancient civilization of Mexico and Central America.
23. A radioactive form of this element is used in dating.
24. Object made by human workmanship.
26. Scrolls dating from the first century BC were discovered near here (2 words).
28. An artificial hill.
29. Important material in Mesopotamia.
30. A monument with a rectangular base and four triangular faces meeting at an apex.
32. A fragment of pottery.
33. Ancient Babylonian king and lawgiver.

Down

2. Rediscovered by Heinrich Schliemann.
3. He discovered the palace at Knossos in Crete.
5. Country where the Parthenon is located.
6. Period in the history of humankind before recorded history.
9. Stone that provided key to decipherment of hieroglyphics.
11. These are good resources for artifacts in civilizations that believed in an afterlife.
15. Advanced Bronze Age civilization in Crete.
16. Pompeii and Herculaneum were destroyed by one.
18. Important material to the Sumerians.
19. A symbol used in the system of writing in ancient Egypt.
22. Their calendar stone was actually a monument to the sun god.
25. Dendrochronology is a dating method using this.
27. Where Great Pyramid of Khufu is located.
31. Pattern of horizontal and vertical lines used as reference for locating points.
34. Ancient city of Sumer, S. Mesopotamia.

Glossary

Anthropologist—A person who studies the origin and the physical, social, and cultural development of human beings.

Antiquary—One who studies or deals in antiquities. Also called an antiquarian.

Antiquities—Objects dating from ancient times.

Archaeology—The systematic recovery and study of material evidence remaining from past human life and culture.

Artifact—An object produced or shaped by human workmanship.

Carbon-14—A naturally radioactive carbon isotope.

Cartouche—In Egyptian hieroglyphics, an oval figure that encloses characters expressing royal or divine names.

Chronology—The determination of dates and the sequence of events. Also called dating.

Civilization—An advanced stage of development, usually used to describe an urban and literate society.

Culture—The behavior, arts, beliefs, institutions and other products and thoughts characteristic of a community.

Cuneiform—The wedge-shaped characters used in ancient Sumerian, Akkadian, Assyrian, Babylonian and Persian writing. Also used to describe the documents written in these characters.

Dendrochronology—The study of the growth rings in trees to date past events.

Dig—An archaeological excavation.

Excavation—The act of digging out.

Fieldwork—The discovery, examination and recording of a site before excavation. (Some archaeologists call all out-of-doors work "fieldwork.")

Hieroglyphics—Pictorial symbols of ancient Egypt used to represent sounds or words. Also called hieroglyphs.

Inscription—Something that is written, printed, carved, engraved or otherwise marked on or in a a surface.

Mound—A hill.

Neolithic—The New Stone Age. (Began about 10,000 BC in the Middle East and later elsewhere. Characterized by the invention of farming and more advanced stone implements.)

Paleolithic—The Old Stone Age. (Began with the earliest chipped stone tools about 750,000 years ago.)

Potsherd—A fragment of broken pottery.

Prehistoric—Pertaining to the era before recorded history.

Pyramid—A monument having a rectangular base and four triangular faces meeting in a single apex; found especially in Egypt, where it served as a tomb.

Stratigraphy—The study of layers of earth.

Stratum—A horizontal layer of material.

Tell—An artificial hill resulting from the accumulation of centuries of human occupation at that spot.

Varve—A layer of sediment.

Ziggurat—A temple tower of the ancient Assyrians and Babylonians having the form of a terraced pyramid.

Answers to Tests, Quizzes and Crossword Puzzle

Pre-Test
1. B
2. A
3. A
4. C
5. A
6. B
7. A
8. D
9. A
10. B

Quiz After Page 11
1. Archaeology
2. Artifacts
3. Culture
4. Mound or hill
5. Stratigraphy
6. Lowest, uppermost (or similar term)
7. Grid
8. Knife, brush, spade, sieve, trowel, etc,
9. Where
10. Potsherds

Quiz After Page 16
1. Tools
2. Prehistory
3. Paleolithic
4. Neolithic
5. Writing, metallurgy
6. Bronze, Iron
7. Dating
8. Dendrochronology
9. Varves
10. Carbon-14

Quiz After Page 29
1. Mummification
2. Tombs
3. Sir Flinders Petrie
4. Rosetta Stone, Jean François Champollion
5. Papyrus
6. Tutankhamen
7. Valley of the Kings
8. Sphinx
9. Nile
10. Dry or arid

Quiz After Page 34
1. Tigris, Euphrates
2. Sumer
3. Clay
4. Cuneiform
5. Behistun Rock
6. Wedge-shaped
7. Paul Botta
8. Ziggurat
9. Sennacherib
10. Ur

Quiz After Page 36
1. Inscriptions or writing
2. Animal bones, tortoise shells
3. Silk
4. Yellow River
5. Great Wall of China

Quiz After Page 47
1. Antiquary (antiquarian)
2. Parthenon
3. Heinrich Schliemann
4. Bronze
5. Minoan
6. Sir Arthur Evans
7. Minotaur
8. Mt. Vesuvius
9. Excellent (or similar term)
10. Roman

Quiz After Page 50
1. England
2. Sarsens
3. Three
4. Druids
5. Worship

Quiz After Page 57
1. Navajo
2. Baskets and other woven items
3. Cliff houses and large community dwellings
4. Mayan
5. John Lloyd Stephens
6. Codices (plural), codex (singular)
7. Sun
8. Inca
9. Machu Picchu
10. Hiram Bingham

Quiz After Page 61
1. Prehistoric cave paintings
2. Dead Sea Scrolls
3. Jacques-Yves Cousteau
4. Observation, Discovery, Recording
5. Diver

Post-Test
1. C
2. D
3. B
4. A
5. B
6. D
7. C
8. A
9. D
10. B

Answers to Word Search

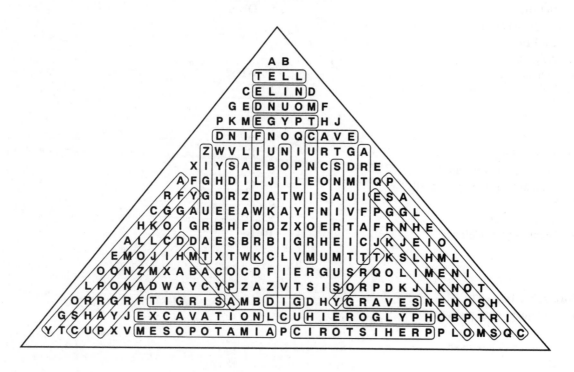

Answers to Crossword Puzzle

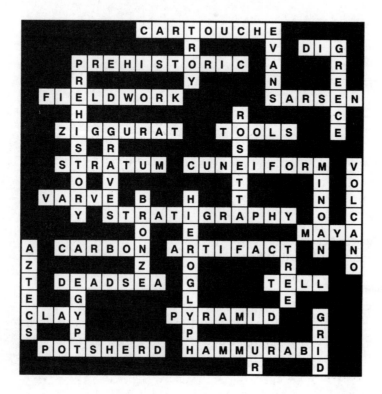

Answers and Background Information to Activities

Excavation (Pages 6–11)
Where to Dig (Pages 6–7)

1. A few examples are the Sphinx, the pyramids of Egypt, the pyramids of Central and South America, Machu Picchu, Stonehenge and the monoliths of Easter Island.

2.

3. The site would be chosen for the same reasons it originally was chosen. Perhaps it was high up and safe from floods, near a wooded area with plentiful game, or near a river well-stocked with fish. Perhaps it was easily defended. After years of being deserted, vegetation would once again grow. When the new settlers arrived at the site, they probably saw the same advantages as the original settlers.

4. The use of aerial photography began as a side effect of military reconnaissance during World War I and was further advanced during World War II. The intelligence agencies of the nations involved hired archaeologists to aid in their photographic missions. A great number of new sites have been discovered by aerial photography.

Many are sites that could not be found on the ground. They show up in aerial photography as variations in the color of the soil and in the density of the crops.

5. Over ruined wall, the growth of the crops is stunted. Over filled-in ditches, deeply rooted crops grow luxuriantly.

6. A proton magnetometer measures weak magnetic forces. Clay contains tiny particles with magnetic properties. When clay is baked, the magnetic properties tend to align along the earth's magnetic field, and the clay becomes a weak magnet. Because the proton magnetometer can detect forces too weak to be detected by a pocket compass, it can help the archaeologist find buried pottery kilns and filled-in pits and ditches.

Resistivity surveying is based upon the principle that electricity flows more readily through some materials than others. For example, it flows more easily through copper than through glass. Another way of saying this would be that copper has low resistance and glass has high resistance. A sharp rise in the resistivity would be an indication of buried masonry or filled-in holes and ditches. If an empty tomb were between the probes, there would be no medium of conduction and would, therefore, offer infinite resistance.

Stratigraphy (Page 8)

1. The layers might be mixed up by plowing, by old objects being inherited by the later folk, or by new objects dropping down—through a hole, for example—to a lower stratum.

Excavation (Page 9)

2. Synonyms for *meticulous* are *conscientious, scrupulous, fastidious, careful,* and *precise.*

Tools (Page 10)

1. Many of the artifacts are very fragile. The worker must be extremely patient and gentle.

2. Such artifacts as beads, pierced shells, and other tiny valuable objects might otherwise be discarded or unnoticed.

3. Under most circumstances, the best thing to do would be to advise the director of the dig of your find. Inexpert handling could destroy the find.

4. Artifacts might give different clues as to their use, history and age according to where they have been found. For example, a pierced sea shell found at an inland site would show that trade was likely carried on with people on the coast.

Potsherds (Page 11)

1. Even in ancient times people tended to throw away their broken pottery and to replace it with the more recent style. That makes it valuable to the archaeologist for dating purposes. Also, because the pottery was easy to make and of little value, it was seldom imported or carried away as booty; therefore, it is usually representative of the site in which it is found.

2. Much of the pottery of the past was decorated with scenes of everyday occurrences. They also decorated their pottery with representations of their gods, goddesses and religious symbols.

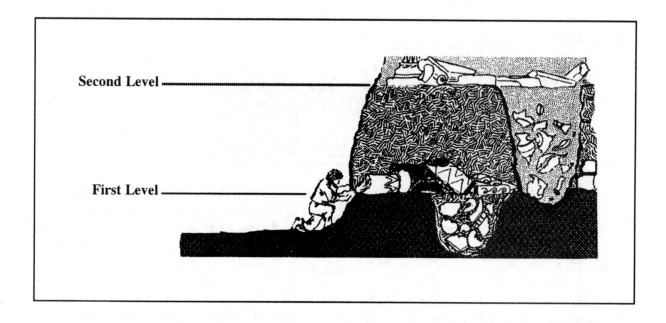

3. The archaeologist might not realize that the tools and potsherds found at the bottom of the pit belong to the more recent town even though those found at the same level outside the pit belong to the older town.

The Ages of Human Existence (Pages 12–13)

1. We are in the Atomic Age or Nuclear Age.

2. There was overlapping, for the ages of civilization did not begin at the same time in all places.

Chronology (Pages 14–16)

1. The experts who might help are as follows:

       Paintings of animals on a cave wall: Paleontologist (3)

       Pottery in which pollen was used to temper clay: Botanist (5)

       A piece of a vase, ground into powder, to be tested for the glow it gives off: Chemist (1)

       A tablet with ancient writing: Linguist (2)

       Human remains left by retreating glacier of last Ice Age: Geologist (4)

2. They are only applicable within a certain time and geographical limit.

3. Papyrus scrolls, a bone knife (although bone does not always test accurately), a wooden beam and the linen cloth could be tested by the carbon-14 method.

4. The beam is about 5,700 years old.

Ancient Egypt (Pages 17–28)
The Pyramids (Pages 17–19)

1.

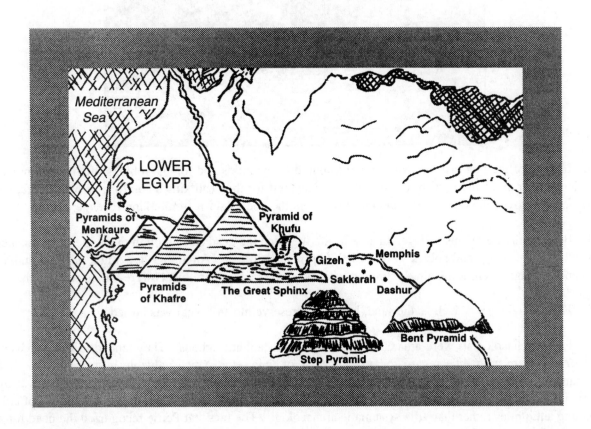

2. The Seven Wonders of the World were first designated by Antipater of Sidon in the second century BC.

   1) The Pyramids of Gizeh were built by Fourth Dynasty Egyptian pharaohs. The Great Pyramid of Khufu was finished *c.* 2580 BC.

   2) The Temple of Artemis of the Ephesians was built *c.* 350 BC. at Ephesus, Turkey.

   3) The tomb of King Mausolus of Caria was built at Halicannassus (now Bodrum), Turkey, *c.* 325 BC.

   4) The Hanging Gardens of Semiramis were built at Babylon, Iraq, *c.* 600 BC.

   5) The 40-foot, marble-gold-and-ivory statue of Zeus was built in the fifth century BC at Olympia, Greece.

   6) The 400-foot-tall lighthouse of Pharos was built by Sostratus of Cnidus off the coast of El Iskandarya (Alexandria), Egypt.

   7) The 117-foot statue of Helios (Apollo), called the Colossus of Rhodes, was sculpted by Chares of Lindus from 292 to 280 BC.

Only the Pyramids remain intact. Of the others, fragments remain of the Temple of Artemis and the Tomb of King Mausolus. No trace remains of the other four.

3. In spite of the fact that men were hired to guard to pyramids and tombs, robbers often broke in and stole some or all of the furnishings and other objects left for the dead king's comfort. What's more, the robbers destroyed the bodies in an attempt to prevent the body's spirit from taking revenge.

4. Because the Egyptians believed in an afterlife in which the dead carried on in much the same manner as when alive, kings and nobles were buried with many artifacts. Anything they might need, including weapons, magnificent furnishings, clothing, chariots, boxes and other objects were buried with them.

5. The arid climate, as well as the sand, helped to preserve most of what was buried.

7. Early archaeologists were amateurs, with crude, self-taught methods. They tended to go after what interested them with little regard for other periods of time, etc. Much valuable information was lost because of this disregard. In the eighteenth and nineteenth centuries most of the work being done was by "dilettantes," the term for those who loved ancient art. In other words, it was more or less the fad of collecting antiquities rather than true systematic archaeology. The fact that Petrie recognized the need for a systematic method of excavation at such a young age was amazing. He is credited with developing just such a method, which he summarized in *Methods and Aims in Archaeology,* published in 1904.

1.

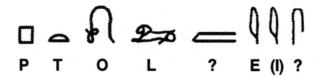

P   T   O   L   ?   E (I) ?

(The Greek spelling was Ptolemaios.)

K   L   E   O   P   A   T   R   A

2. Champollion suggested that the Egyptian language might have had characters that looked different but sounded the same.

3. In our alphabet we have several sets of letters which look different but which sometimes have similar sounds: *c* and *s, c* and *k,* and *g* and *j.*

5. Many Greeks had come to Egypt in the fourth century BC. They were mostly mercenaries and traders. The Greek population in Egypt grew by large numbers after Alexander founded the city of Alexandria. When Egypt became part of Alexander's empire, one of his generals, Ptolemy I, was put in charge of Egypt and founded the Ptolemaic Dynasty. Greek-speaking Ptolemies were still in power at the time the Rosetta Stone was written. In fact, the inscription summarized the benefactions conferred by Ptolemy Epiphanes (205–180 BC).

6. The following are the steps in making papyrus:
    1. Remove the fibrous layers within the stem of the papyrus plant.
    2. Place the layers side by side.
    3. Cross the first set of layers with another set of layers set at right angles.
    4. Dampen the sheet.
    5. Press the sheet.
    6. Allow the sheet to dry.

Upon drying, the glue-like sap of the plant acted as an adhesive and cemented the layers together.

7. The Greek text could be read by scholars. It stated clearly that the document was set for the same text in all three scripts. Even with the Greek text, the decipherment was a long and arduous task. Without the Greek text, it would have been close to impossible.

9. It was the triple inscription of the Rosetta Stone which made it possible to decipher hieroglyphics. The decipherment laid the foundation of modern Egyptology. The work of Thomas Young and Jean François Champollion established the basis for the translation of all future Egyptian hieroglyphic texts.

The Tomb of King Tutankhamen (Pages 25–28)
1. Included among the details on each card were position, description (minute details, including colors), dimensions and an illustration.

2. In 1907 a previous excavator with whom Carter had worked had found several jars of baked clay which had seal impressions with the name Tutankhamen. Carter also knew that a small pit-tomb with other artifacts bearing Tutankhamen's name had been found. Although others believed these things to be all that remained, Howard Carter did not. He was convinced that the real tomb of Tutankhamen was unaccounted for and that it was to be found in the general area of where this previous evidence had been found.

7. The following are synonyms for *perseverance*: *persistence, tenacity, steadfastness,* and *stick-to-itiveness.*

Mesopotamia (Pages 30–34)
1. The modern name for the region is Iraq.

2. The inscription had been chiselled in the wall of a 1,700-foot cliff. Rawlinson dangled from a rope about 500 feet above ground to get close enough to transcribe the Old Persian and Elamite portions. That took about two years. He could not get close enough to the Babylonian portion, but several years later he found a native boy who agreed to climb to the inscription and make a squeeze of it. (A squeeze is a cast in wet pulped paper.)

3. The buildings were made of mud-brick; therefore, they were very vulnerable to the weather and in constant need of repair. The layers of settlement (occupation) that built up formed the mound, or tell.

6. The evidence suggested a possible correlation with the deluge described in Genesis. The story would have been passed on through the Assyrians and Babylonians to the Jews.

7. Our systems of time and angles are based on the number 60.

Ancient China (Pages 35–36)

2. Although all the spoken languages are not understood, the written language can be understood by all.

4. The following is how silk is made:
   1. Pick the leaves from the mulberry trees.
   2. Keep the silkworms together on shelves, allowing them to feed on the mulberry leaves.
   3. Wait as each of the worms produces a fine silk thread which forms a cocoon.
   4. Soak the threads in hot water.
   5. Lift out each thread with chopsticks and wind it on a reel.
   6. Twist the threads into strands on a spinning machine.
   7. Dye the threads.
   8. On a hand loom, weave the threads together into solid or colored patterns.
   9. Pound the woven silk to make it soft.
   10. Iron the silk flat.

5. Uses of silk were clothing (for the wealthy), a medium for painting and writing material (before the invention of paper).

6. They are all in the flood plain of a great river. The rich deposits of alluvial soil and the supply of fresh water to irrigate the crops and support animal life provided the potential for producing food.

8. By the time of the Chou Dynasty (1027 BC), the states of China had thick walls and watchtowers along the northern borders. But when the First Emperor of China came into power, he saw that China was still open to invasion by Asian tribes from the north; therefore, he issued the order to join all the existing walls into one great one.

Ancient Greece (Pages 37–43)

2. In 1764 the English Society of Dilettanti sent out the first organized expedition in the history of archaeology. Greece became a favorite spot for eighteenth- and nineteenth-century collectors. While under Turkish rule nothing was done to protect its monuments. Lord Elgin, the British ambassador to Turkey in the early nineteenth century, collected many of the Parthenon sculptures, which otherwise might have been destroyed. The so-called "Elgin Marbles" are among the most beautiful artifacts of the ancient world.

The Discovery of Troy (Pages 38–40)

1.

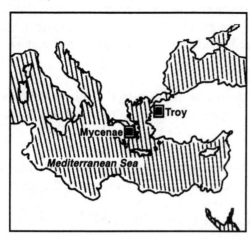

2. Schliemann knew that Homer's Troy was very ancient. He assumed that since the Troy described by Homer had been destroyed about 3,000 years earlier, it would be deep in the mound. He knew that the lowest level, which did not contain bronze, could not be Homer's Troy, for Homer had so often mentioned bronze spears and swords. At that time neither Schliemann nor others of his time had any idea that a great Bronze Age civilization had existed in the area.

3. According to legend, the goddess Eris, or Discord, was in a fury over not having been invited to a wedding. Knowing the trouble it would cause, she threw into the midst of the guests an apple with the inscription "to the fairest." Hera, Aphrodite, and Athene each thought it should be hers. Zeus instructed a shepherd named Paris to make the judgment. Hera offered Paris kingly power if he would choose her; Athene offered him military power; and Aphrodite offered him the love of the most beautiful woman alive. Paris accepted Aphrodite's offer. The most beautiful woman alive was Helen, wife of Menelaus, king of Sparta. According to the legend, Paris's seduction of Helen, with the help of Aphrodite, and his refusal to let her go led to the start of the Trojan War.

4. Schliemann and Columbus both set out to make spectacular discoveries. Neither found (at first) what he was looking for, but both found something even more extraordinary.

Pompeii and Herculaneum (Pages 41–44)

1.

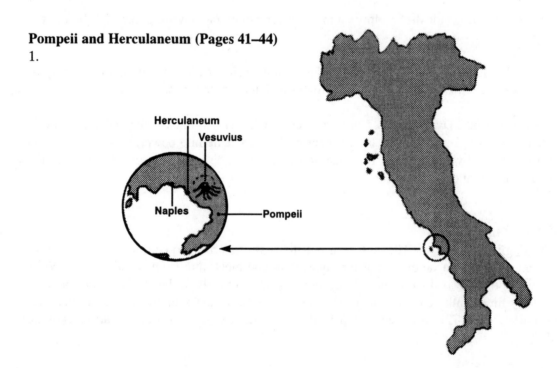

2. What makes it strange that these towns were forgotten is the fact that the disaster occurred long after written history began. Records of the disaster did exist.

4. The Romans did not want any reminders of times when they were not under Roman rule.

5. Scholars had not previously believed religion to play such an important role in people's lives during that period of time.

The Minoans (Pages 45–47)

2. King Minos, the legendary ruler of Crete, was the son of Zeus and Europa. He defeated Athens and Megara as revenge for the killing of his son Androgeos by the Athenians. According to legend, Minos kept the Minotaur, half bull and half man, in the Labyrinth, built for that purpose by Daedalus. To further avenge the death of his son, Minos demanded that seven young Athenian youths and maidens be sent every nine months (in another version, every year) to the Labyrinth as sacrifices to the Minotaur. After a few years, the Athenian hero Theseus, with the help of Minos's daughter Ariadne, killed the creature.

The legend may have been connected with the bull-leaping ceremony, possibly a sacred rite.

3. Built around 2000 BC, the palace at Knossus spread over six acres of land with heights reaching over four stories. It was built in a labyrinth, maze-like pattern and provided housing for about 100,000 people!

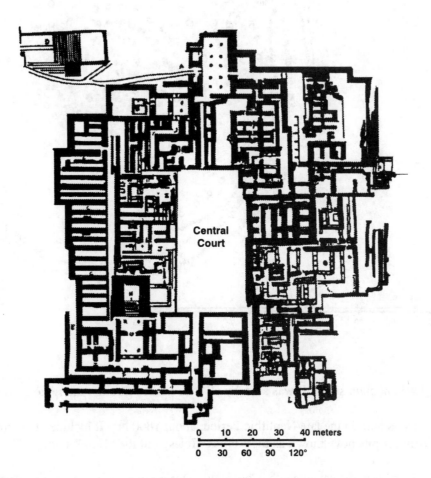

5. Heinrich Schliemann discovered at least nine layers of separate cultures at Troy. Arthur Evans found a different set of circumstances at Knossos. The ruins were all in one layer. Each set of occupants built onto the existing structure. They tore down sections of the old only when necessary. This seems to suggest one long, continuous occupation, as opposed to the intermittent cultures at Troy.

6. Two types of pottery were characteristic of the Minoans: Gray Minyan, which gets its name from the Minyan tribe at Orchomenos in Boetia, where the artifacts were first found, and matt-painted were. The Gray Minyan pottery was angular in shape and had a metallic-like appearance. The matt-painted ware was pale green with black, linear-patterned decorations.

7. There are always problems concerning what to do with excavated structures. Should they be recovered? Should they be preserved? Should they be restored? Should the art treasures of ancient Greece and Egypt be taken out of western museums and be returned to their countries of origin?

Stonehenge (Pages 48–50)

1.

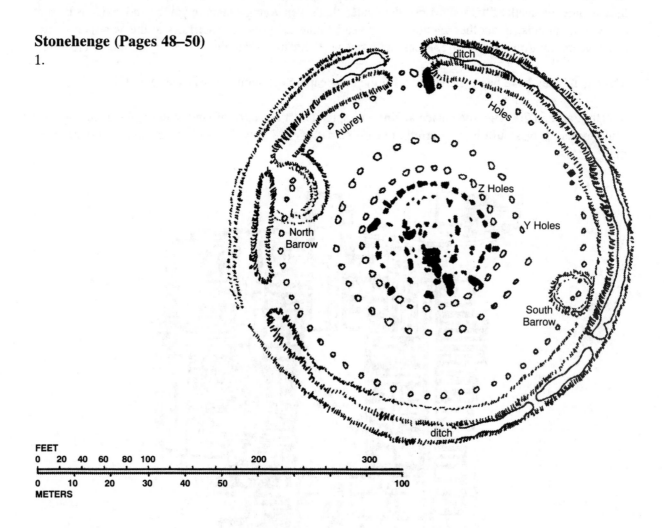

2. Stonehenge was in plain sight. It was seen by all who passed through the region.

3. Stonehenge I was built in the late Neolithic Period, about 1800 BC. It included the outer circular ditch and bank; the fifty-six pits now known as the Aubrey Holes; and the "Hele" stone, a 35-ton sarsen.

Stonehenge II was built in the seventeenth century BC. During this phase, two concentric circles of bluestones, transported from Wales, were erected in the center of the site. But the double circle was never completed and was later dismantled.

Stonehenge III was worked upon about 1600 BC. About eighty sarsens were brought in and set up in a circle in the following manner: thirty uprights topped by a continuous ring of stone lintels. Enclosed in the circle was a horseshoe formation of five trilithons—each consisting of a pair of uprights supporting a stone lintel. Shortly thereafter about twenty bluestones from Phase II were dressed and set down upon an oval setting. Then the oval structure was taken down and the bluestones and those stones dismantled from Phase II were rearranged.

4. Modern archaeology as a science is less than two centuries old. The sixteenth-century Italian Renaissance brought about a new enthusiasm for the arts and classical learning. Those who eagerly collected antiques, such as the artifacts long buried in Italian gardens, are called antiquarians. The antiquarians were mostly interested in finding valuable objects. They paid little attention to common objects, which modern archaeologists would value for what they teach about ancient cultures. In fact, in the course of their excavations, the antiquarians destroyed much of value in terms of modern archaeology. It must be remembered, nevertheless, that it was was out of this fad for collecting antiquities that the science of archaeology was born.

6. Atkinson, Piggot and Stone unselfishly left the other half alone in the knowledge that some day archaeologists would have better equipment with which to study and date their finds.

Earliest Americans (Pages 51–57)
The Anasazi (Pages 51–52)
1. The artifacts found in the oldest strata were so well made that archaeologists assumed they could not have been made by beginners. As no cultural or physical evidence has ever been found of previous homes, the archaeologists further concluded that a simpler Basket Maker culture existed as nomadic hunters and natural food gatherers who took refuge in temporary crude shelters and caves.

3. *Anasazi* is Navajo for "Ancient Ones."

4. Some scholars believe that the move resulted partly from the pressure of nomadic Navajos and Apaches from the north and partly from a severe drought that plagued the region from 1276 to 1299.

The Maya (Pages 53–54)
1. The principal crop was maize.

2. The Yucatán is an extremely dry area. The southern region is a rainforest area.

4. The Classic Period of the Mayan civilization was from *c.* AD 300–900. A characteristic feature of this period was the custom of erecting carved monuments called stelae at the end of every twenty-year period. The ancient Maya prayed to the gods and offered them food, drink and incense to please them. The priests held an extremely important position in Mayan society. They decided when conditions were favorable for undertakings such as building or hunting. They were administrators, scholars, architects, astronomers and teachers. Probably the most original aspect of the Mayan religion was the advanced level of mathematical and astronomical knowledge. This knowledge included two brilliant discoveries: positional numeration and zero. Their achievements in astronomy were just as great. They calculated the duration of the solar year with extreme accuracy. The basis for their calendar was a 260-day sacred year, called *tzolkin*. The priests, of course, were the only ones who could interpret the calendar. The ancient Maya were among the few peoples known to have worshiped time.

5. Sample codex:

6. When the Spaniards conquered the Maya and other native peoples, they destroyed their writings, which were in the form of books we now call codices. Each codex was in the form of brightly-colored picture writing. The codices contained not only the history of the people, but also their treatment of diseases, ceremonies of magic, and their ideas about astronomy. The Spanish priests were convinced that in order to spread Christianity, they must completely rid these people of their beliefs. Seeing these codices as an important part of the Mayan culture, the first bishop of Yucatán had the codices burned. Of the many codices once in existence, only four survived the destruction and these have been difficult to decipher. Perhaps if more had survived, the task would have been easier. If the Spaniards had not ordered the destruction of these valuable documents, we would have been able to learn a great deal more about the native cultures of Central and South America.

The Aztec Calendar (Page 55)
1. The Aztec Calendar is a stone sculpture with a 13-foot diameter. Although known as the Aztec Calendar Stone, it is actually a monument to the sun god. The design does include the signs for the twenty named days of the week, but most of the symbols represent the sun.

The Inca (Pages 56–57)
1.

2. Machu Picchu is located about fifty miles northwest of Cuzco. It went unnoticed by the Spaniards because of its position high in a narrow saddle between two sharp mountain peaks. It is one of the few pre-Columbian urban centers still nearly intact. The site covers about five square miles and includes a temple and a citadel. At one time these structures were surrounded by terraced gardens with more than 2,000 steps.

Accidental Finds (Pages 58–60)

1.

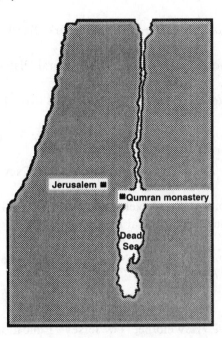

2. Farmers plowing fields, construction workers clearing the ground for buildings or roads, and soldiers are among those who might unearth artifacts by chance.

4. Most of the paintings were put there for religious reasons. The ceremonies usually included magic, which was carried out in dark places.

6. Ancient books had to be copied by hand; therefore, there was a high probability of error. Seldom were two copies of a book exactly alike: there were many mistakes in spelling; words might be out of order; and entire lines might be repeated, left out, or put in the wrong place. Later copyists often made things worse by trying to correct the errors.

Underwater Archaeology (Page 61)

1. Underwater archaeology first developed in the twentieth century. The aqualung invented by Cousteau is the type most commonly used. Cousteau's work at Le Grand Congloue near Marseille and Peter Throckmorton's and George Bass's work off the coast of southern Turkey were important pioneering underwater excavations.

2. The following words make up the acronym *scuba:*

S elf
C ontained
U nderwater
B reathing
A pparatus

Bibliography

BOOKS

Benjamin, Nora. *The First Book of Archaeology.* New York: Franklin Watts, 1957.

Cottrell, Leonard. *Lost Civilizations.* London: Franklin Watts International, 1974.

Freeman, Mae Blacker. *Finding out about the Past.* New York: Random House, 1967.

Garnett, Henry. *Treasures of Yesterday.* New York: The Natural History Press, 1964.

Glubok, Shirley. *Art and Archeology.* New York: Harper and Row, 1966.

Higgins, Reynold. *The Archaeology of Minoan Crete.* New York: Henry Z. Walck, 1973.

Holden, Raymond. *Secrets in the Dust: The Story of Archeology.* New York: Dodd, Mead, 1959.

McAlpine, Jim and Marion Finkbinder, Sue Jeweler, and Betty Weincek. *As It Was! Ancient Africa.* Hawthorne, New Jersey: Educational Impressions, 2001.

_____. *As It Was! Ancient Egypt.* Hawthorne, New Jersey: Educational Impressions, 2001.

_____. *As It Was! Ancient Greece.* Hawthorne, New Jersey: Educational Impressions, 2001.

_____. *As It Was! Ancient Rome.* Hawthorne, New Jersey: Educational Impressions, 2001.

National Geographic Society. *Clues to America's Past.* Washington, D.C.: National Geographic Society, 1969.

Silverberg, Robert. *Lost Cities and Vanished Civilizations.* Philadelphia: Chilton House, 1962.

_____. *Seven Wonders of the Ancient World.* New York: The Macmillan Company, 1970.

White, Anne Terry. *All About Archaeology.* New York: Random House, 1959.

VIDEOCASSETTES

Ancient Greece. Hawthorne, New Jersey: January Productions, 1992.

Ancient Rome. Hawthorne, New Jersey: January Productions, 1992.

Seven Wonders of the Ancient World. Chicago: Questar Video, Inc., 1973.